ENGLISH ART POTTERY 1865-1915

I   Vase, stoneware. Doulton and Co., decorated by Frank Butler. Height 15¼ins. Circa 1900.

ENGLISH
ART POTTERY
1865-1915

by Malcolm Haslam

Antique Collectors' Club

ISBN 0-902028 26 X

NK
4085
.E46
1975

Printed in England by Baron Publishing,
Church Street, Woodbridge, Suffolk.

Contents

Preface

To write an account of an artistic movement which occurred in England round the turn of the century, is necessarily to draw on the wealth of documentary material provided by the numerous art-magazines of that era. Rather than repeatedly quote from these sources, it seemed wiser to reprint some of the most interesting articles in full, or at length. The tone of the contemporary author, often unrecognizable in short quotations, can be more enlightening than the hard facts he committed to paper.

It is hoped that the reader will catch from the reprinted material a period flavour which any modern author would find it hard to infuse. An account of William De Morgan's lustre pottery written in 1876, despite the writer's archaic turn of phrase, portrays more vividly the impact of the new ware than the historian, writing nearly a hundred years later, can hope to do; and the immediacy of a potter's own words, when he describes his achievements and his aspirations, is often far more revealing than the mere record of his work. In the introduction, I have tried to augment the factual information where possible, to enlarge on the stylistic context, and to give a historical perspective which no contemporary writer could have done.

In the selection of illustrations, the aim has been to show the work of as many potteries as possible — not necessarily the best work, but typical examples — and to avoid reproducing illustrations that have already been widely published. I am grateful to Mr. Ian Bennett for allowing me to illustrate pieces from his collection which appear in figures 22, 64, 65, 109, 134, 159, 166, 167, 170, 189 and colour plate XIV. My thanks are also due to Messrs. Richard Dennis, Andy Tilbrook, Rowena Fitzgerald, John Scott, Albert Gallichan and Peter Rose.

Malcolm Haslam
London, 1975

The Art Pottery Movement

The story told in this book is one of revival. By the second half of the nineteenth century, ceramics as a means of artistic expression had all but perished in England, the victim of industrial production and bad taste. The artist-potters treated these maladies, and gradually, over the fifty years between 1865 and 1915, a healthy organism emerged. Bad taste persisted, and industrial production remained the most economic method of producing the crockery which England has always exported in large quantities. But, by 1915, there was a public who would pay for pottery because it was beautiful and made by hand; the potter had come to be recognised as an individual artist and the ceramic medium was considered a valid means of artistic expression; and art-school *curricula* had begun to include pottery classes. Soon after the First World War, artist-potters' work was being exhibited at West End art galleries.

It is difficult to make qualitative judgements about public taste, and future generations may not share our opinion of the progress of design in nineteenth-century England. But from the 1830s there was a growing clamour against the style, or lack of style, of the artefacts which industry produced. Men directly concerned with national art-education, which was introduced in 1836, tried to formulate a rationale of good design under three main heads: form, which should be independent of ornament, should relate to the purpose of the object and the material in which it was to be manufactured; ornament should emphasise form, rather than obscure it; and with regard to both form and ornament, the best results were to be achieved by studying and assimilating, but not imitating, Nature and the great styles of the past. This was the message of *The Journal of Design and Manufacture,* edited by Henry Cole, which appeared between 1849 and 1852, and it was the onus of Richard Redgrave's unfavourable report on the Great Exhibition of 1851. The same principles were enshrined in William Dyce's *Introduction to the Drawing-book of the School of Design* (published 1854) and Owen Jones's *The Grammar of Ornament* (1856), two manuals which were the basis of art-school teaching well into the twentieth century.

The effects of the new dogma were not immediately apparent, to any degree, in ceramics. Henry Cole designed a tea-set for Minton's which was plain and elegant and which won an award from the Society of Arts. Minton's also produced decorated tableware to designs by the neo-Gothic architect A.W.N. Pugin, whose books on architecture and ornament had influenced the reformers. Although this pottery represented an oasis in the desert of mid-nineteenth century ceramics, it was still industrial and functional.

During the 1850s, John Ruskin became convinced of the inherent ugliness of objects produced in modern factories. For his book *The Stones of Venice* he made an intensive study of the city's Gothic architecture and sculpture. He thought that they had become less beautiful as the government of the city had passed from the masses to the few. The tyrannical Doges of Renaissance Venice corresponded in his mind to the capitalist factory-owners of modern Britain. Workers could not produce beautiful things if they were enslaved. In a chapter of *The Stones of Venice* entitled 'The Nature of Gothic' he claimed that if the freedom and orignality of the craftsman were sacrificed to the modern desire for 'engine-turned precision' his work would lack the imagination and spontaneity characteristic of the best Gothic art.

Ruskin's writings created a wide public who would regard the imperfections of handiwork, not as a drawback, but rather as the hallmark of artistic integrity. Many would purchase crude Doulton stoneware rather than elegant Wedgwood china whose consciences were troubled by the deplorable conditions which prevailed in the factories of Victorian England.

In 1861, with the foundation of Morris, Marshall, Faulkner and Co., Ruskin's philosophy was put into practice. Furniture, metalwork, stained glass and embroidered hangings were produced by hand and marketed through 'the Firm's' showroom in Oxford Street. Some Dutch tiles were painted to designs by D.G. Rossetti, Albert Moore, Simeon Solomon and William De Morgan, but otherwise the manufacture of ceramics was not undertaken. From 1864, C. Eastlake was writing essays for the fashionable periodicals, in which he criticised the industrial furnishings offered by the decorating trade and warmly recommended simpler, handmade artefacts, produced in rural areas or by less developed nations, which were to be purchased cheaply in bric-a-brac shops. In 1868, these essays were collected together and published with the title *Hints on Household Taste,* the first of a plethora of manuals of interior decoration which appeared during the Aesthetic Movement. Oscar Wilde, the Movement's high priest and the arbiter of good taste until his downfall in 1895, publicised the idea of surrounding oneself with objects of beauty which were to be contemplated for their purely aesthetic merits, rather than to indicate the wealth and culture of their owner.

An upshot of the Aesthetic Movement was a greater appreciation of Oriental ceramics. Rossetti, Whistler and other artists at the centre of the Movement collected 'blue and white', but in the last two decades of the century museums and collectors were purchasing examples of work by Chinese and Japanese potters in a wide variety of decorative techniques.

In these circumstances, a demand was created for pottery which was handmade and appealed to the eye through its form and decoration, to meet which the organisation of the ceramics industry was ill-fitted and had to be modified. In general, one of three systems was adopted: established factories, such as Wedgwood's, Doulton's and Minton's opened studios where outside artists were employed to decorate wares produced by the normal industrial processes: small factories were started which were operated more like studio-workshops, where potters with industrial experience supplied the technical expertise: an artist, with more or less ceramic training, set up on his own, or with a few assistants, and carried out all or most of the manufacturing and decorating processes himself. In the last system, the artist-potter, in the twentieth-century sense, has emerged.

There were artist-potters in France before one appeared in England. Charles Avisseau, a trained ceramist, had started to make and decorate his own *faience* at Tours in 1829. In 1839, the painter Jules-Claude Ziegler, when he found his eyesight failing, had turned to pottery and started making artistic stoneware at Voisinlieu in the Oise. Théodore Deck, trained as a modeller, set up his own pottery-studio at Paris in 1856. French precedents were important to the Martin brothers, when they set up on their own in 1877, and as late as 1894 a writer in *The Studio* was recommending the practice of French artist-potters such as Delaherche and Bigot, and regretting that it was hardly known in England.

The notion of artist as craftsman, in the nineteenth century, originated with the Nazarenes, a group of German painters working in Rome. They identified themselves with the anonymous artisans of the Middle Ages. The Pre-Raphaelite painters had assimilated this idea, along with others, from the Germans. Ruskin's theorising on Gothic art led him to condemn the division of labour, the ideal of economic efficiency proposed by Adam Smith in 1776, and quickly put into practice by Josiah Wedgwood. If the roles of the artist and craftsman were to be performed by one man, it follows that he would have to be both. This was an attractive proposition to the many young European painters and sculptors in the second half of the nineteenth century who were bored by the aridity of their training and discontented with the conventional styles in which they were expected to work. In 1894, the Belgian artist Henry van de Velde, who became one of the leading designers of Art Nouveau,

II   Jug, stoneware. Martin Brothers. Height 8ins. Dated 1874.

wrote: 'Oh, if only the academies would establish workshops for weaving, embroidery, lace-work, and for goldsmithing and printing, besides their studios for painting and sculpture. If only they would reveal the secrets of pottery!'

Knowledge of ceramic techniques became more accessible in England as the second half of the nineteenth century progessed. By introducing artists into the factories, the professional potters first permitted outsiders a glimpse of their arcana. English artist-potters were able to benefit from the lectures and advice of Professor Sir Arthur Church F.R.S., whose profound knowledge of ceramic chemistry he freely shared with any who consulted him. In 1880, Church gave the Cantor lectures at the Society of Arts on the subject *Some points of contact between the scientific and artistic aspects of pottery and porcelain.* Papers read to the Society of Arts by the artist-potters themselves (some of which are reprinted in this book) were another source of information and inspiration. Gradually, technical manuals appeared: Richard Lunn's *Pottery, a handbook of practical pottery for art teachers and students* was published in 1903; in the same year Taxile Doat's *Grand Feu Ceramics* began to appear in the American periodical *Keramic Studio;* and in 1914 came *Pottery for Artists, Craftsmen and Teachers* by George Cox. Richard Lunn taught the first formal pottery course in England at the Royal College of Art from 1903, and by 1914 there were classes at the Blackheath and Camberwell art schools.

The development of art pottery over fifty years between 1865 and 1915 was determined by alterations in public taste, in artistic attitudes and in art-education which were so radical that the picture which emerged at the end of the period, so totally different from that at the outset, has since been given only minor touching-up.

Artistic Stoneware

In 1865, George Tinworth, a young sculptor trained at the Lambeth school of art and the Royal Academy Schools, was provided with studio space in Henry Doulton's pottery at Lambeth. At first he worked on terracotta medallions after Classical coins and gems, but by the end of 1866 was decorating artistic stoneware. About thirty pieces by Tinworth and W. Christian Symons were shown at the Paris Exhibition of 1867.

John Sparkes, in the paper he read to the Society of Arts in 1874 (reprinted on p.33), tells how from this beginning the production of 'Lambeth stoneware' expanded and prospered. He says less, however, about the circumstances in which the new enterprise had been undertaken. Sparkes, who had been appointed headmaster of the Lambeth school of art in 1854, made his first approach to Doulton in 1856. At that time Doulton's were the leading manufacturers of industrial, sanitary and domestic stoneware, but they had made no attempt to enter the field of decorative pottery. Sparkes was rebuffed. In 1859, Edward Cresy, an architect friend of Henry Doulton and a medievalist, suggested that the pottery might manufacture some imitations of the Rhenish stoneware (*grès de flandres*) made in the Middle Ages. Cresy had acquired an example of this ware which he showed to Doulton. The latter, however, was dubious about the technical feasibility of such an undertaking. It was not until 1862 that he allowed a trial piece, an inkwell, to be made. Although his earlier reservations were justified, for the cobalt blue introduced into the incised decoration had fled in firing, the piece found its place on the Doulton stand at the International Exhibition of 1862.

Henry Doulton once remarked that 'it was in great measure owing to the stimuli of international exhibitions, and the desire to exhibit something creditable to his country that this manufacture had been developed.' He went on to express his pleasure in having been able to provide 'those who had the artist spirit in them' with 'work in which there was some joy'. These remarks are flavoured with Ruskinian philosophy. Art and architecture, Ruskin maintained, were a matter of national ethics. His declamations were made in the style of evangelical outbursts, and Henry Doulton, a Dissenter married to a Dissenting preacher's daughter, a factory-owner who was also a humanitarian, would have been susceptible to the substance and the form of the critic's message. So, Sparkes's second approach to Doulton, in 1863, met with more positive response.

The opportunity for co-operation between the art school and the pottery arose in 1864 when Doulton built an extension to the Lambeth works. He asked Sparkes to provide busts of Wedgwood, Palissy and other great potters for the facade; these were the 'certain heads which were modelled in the Art School' to which Sparkes refers in his paper. The next year Doulton suggested to Sparkes that Tinworth should start working in the pottery.

An early technical problem was the development of colours which would withstand the temperature of 1250° centigrade required to fuse the clay body and vaporise the salt for glazing, and Doulton was glad to have the advice of Professor Church. Salt-glazed stoneware has one great advantage as an artistic medium. The artist is permitted to work directly on the soft clay, and, to a large extent the decoration retains personal expression through the firing process. The salt glaze does not diminish clarity of detail, and enables the artist to achieve effects through a subtlety and intricacy of incised line which would be almost obliterated by a thicker vitreous glaze. The best example of this is the early work of Hannah Barlow, whose incised animals have the freshness and spontaneity that they would have had on the page of a sketching-block (figure 1). Too often this quality was sacrificed at Doulton's to the pursuit of more elaborate decoration. In particular, the application of florets, beads and other ornament in white slip, no doubt inspired by *grès de flandres,* is to be regretted. Pâte-sur-pâte, although representing a high degree of craftsmanship, has less artistic effect on stoneware than on porcelain, where its delicacy is matched by the body to which it is applied.

The clarity and expressive quality of salt-glazed stoneware make it suitable for modelling. George Tinworth's plaques and figure-groups are to be counted among the best sculpture produced in England at that time (figure 2); Mark V. Marshall is another artist whose modelling is remarkable for its expression and vitality (figures 3 and 4). John Broad and, later, Leslie Harradine were modellers of distinction who worked for Doulton.

Until 1882 each example of artistic stoneware produced at Doulton's was original and unique. From 1882 some designs were produced in series by assistants; these are marked with an impressed 'X' followed by a number. The style of decoration developed according to technical accomplishment and the prevailing artistic taste (figures 5-11). Earlier pieces are medieval in feeling, their decoration either derived from *grès de flandres* or reflecting the geometric style of ornament developed by neo-Gothic designers such as Pugin and Talbert. Other examples are decorated in the fifteenth-century Italian Renaissance style which was widespread in English ceramics during the late 1860s and '70s. Motifs and compositional effects derived from Japanese art are found on many pieces made during the 1870s and '80s.

Both the Gothic and the Japanese elements tended towards a proto-Art Nouveau, particularly marked in the work of Eliza Simmance (figure 12), Frank Butler (colour plate I), and Mark V. Marshall. But by 1900 the style of many of the decorators had generally become more self-conscious, either imitating the work of the Glasgow designers, or following the trend of Continental Art Nouveau (figure 13). Some developments in Doulton stoneware after 1900 are described in a later section.

Other types of stoneware produced at Doulton's were Silicon (figures 14-16), Chiné and Carrara. Silicon has a smooth body of a light buff colour and a very slight glaze. Its decoration was often in the Japanese taste, usually brushed on in black outline with areas of powder-blue slurry, and sometimes painted with white slip; gilding was frequent. It seems to have been introduced *circa* 1881. Chiné was the name given to a type of decoration where a textured surface was obtained by pressing moistened lace or other fabric into the soft clay; it was jointly patented by Doulton and John Slater (who became art director at Doulton's Burslem factory in 1887) and was introduced *circa* 1886. Carrara was a dense white body resembling marble which was decorated with painting and gilding.

Not all Doulton stoneware is of great ceramic or artistic merit. The majority of the decorators were recruited from the Lambeth School of Art and only a few had more than an art school talent for design. Fewer still had any great feeling for the medium. However, good examples of work by the better artists rate high in the context of European and American ceramics of that era. Great significance lay in the way the manufacture was organised. For the first time in nineteenth-century England artists were encouraged to use their own imagination in the decoration of pottery; they were allowed to sign their work by incising their initials in the soft clay. This promoted the concept of a piece of pottery as a work of art.

It was important, too, that the artists at Doulton's worked closely with professional potters. The Martin brothers were some of the first to take advantage of the opportunity to learn ceramic techniques which was provided at Lambeth. In an article in *The Magazine of Art* of 1882 (reprinted on p.48), Cosmo Monkhouse relates in some detail Robert Wallace Martin's early career as a sculptor, and tells how, when he was working as a modeller at Bailey's Fulham pottery, his younger brothers were decorating at Doulton's; and J.F.

III   Vase, stoneware. Martin Brothers. Height 7¼ins. Circa 1890.

Blacker (*The ABC of English Salt-glaze Stoneware,* 1922) wrote: 'They [Walter and Edwin Martin] were very keen on acquiring a practical knowledge of pottery in all its branches. No sooner did the potter leave his wheel when one or the other would jump into his place and "spin" with all his might.'

The commercial success of Doulton's artistic stoneware was significant; it encouraged other firms to follow the lead of Doulton and Sparkes. In Lambeth, at the potteries of George Smith and James Stiff, stoneware was manufactured which was close in style, but only rarely comparable in quality to the Doulton product. Doulton's took over the Stiff works in 1913. At the Fulham Pottery, C.J.C. Bailey undertook production of artistic stoneware (figures 17-21) and *circa* 1872 the *émigré* French landscape-painter and artist-potter Jean-Charles Cazin was made art director. Before coming to England, Cazin had been principal of the art school at Tours, where Avisseau and other artist-potters had, for fifty years, been working in the manner of Bernard Palissy, the sixteenth century French ceramist.

Developments in France had had repercussions in England. It would be ingenuous to suppose that Sparkes and Doulton had not been aware of J.-C. Ziegler's stoneware. Minton's, under the supervision of their French art director Léon Arnoux, had begun making 'Palissy Ware' soon after the Great Exhibition of 1851 at which Avisseau's work had been on display. Several Minton pieces were cast from models by French sculptors. Cazin brought the Tours tradition not only to Fulham, but also to Lambeth, where, through the influence of his friend Alphonse Legros, he was appointed to the staff of the art school. Very little of Cazin's work at Fulham seems to have survived, but the influence of the Tours potters is clearly discernible in the work of Edgar Kettle (figures 17 and 18); at Doulton's, W. Cund, an artist about whom little is known, worked in a style clearly influenced by Cazin. But the Frenchman's most important contribution to English art pottery was the encouragement and instruction he gave to the Martin brothers.

Walter and Edwin Martin were among Cazin's pupils at the Lambeth School of Art, and when he returned to France in 1874 Cazin left his throwing-wheel to Robert Wallace Martin, his colleague at Fulham. Some early pieces by the Martin brothers reflect the Palissy-esque influence of Cazin, and Mark V. Marshall, who before he went to Doulton's, in 1880, worked with the Martins, also shows signs of the same influence (figure 4).

The Martin brothers were the first complete artist-potters in England; they created and decorated their own pottery in a studio-workshop, in the tradition of the French artist-potters. By the time they left Fulham, Walter had learnt to throw successfully, and, unlike the artists at Doulton's, they were no longer dependent on an industrial concern for the technical processes of manufacture (figures 22-27, colour plates II and III).

Although Robert Wallace was generally the modeller, Edwin the decorator, and Walter the thrower, chemist and kiln supervisor, they each performed the tasks of the others on occasion. From the start, their work was strikingly original, sometimes eccentric and highly individual. They escaped the mannerisms of Doulton stoneware, and although lacking the resources of a large factory, developed through years of trial and error considerable technical expertise. Firing the kiln was always primitive and problematical; their ware was directly exposed to the flames at a temperature of 1450° centigrade. Nevertheless, they broadened their colour range until it included blues, greens, yellows, browns, blacks, tortoise-shell and coral-red. Some of their work was thrown or modelled by hand, although plaster moulds were used for many pieces.

The artistic style of early Martinware either reflects the influence of Cazin or *gres de flandres* (colour plate II). From about the time they moved to their works in Southall (found for them by their patron Frederick Nettlefold, who also took the lease on the shop in Holborn which became their showroom and was run by a fourth brother, Charles), they began to decorate their ware with incised ornament in the style of the German Renaissance (figure 23). They also began to include Japanese motifs in their repertoire (figure 24), and the fishes, dragons, birds, insects and plants incised by Edwin on many pieces of the 1880s and '90s were inspired by illustrations in Japanese wood-block printed books which they possessed (figure 25 and colour plate III). Throughout the years of their production, Robert Wallace Martin modelled grotesque birds (which were usually tobacco jars with the bird's head as the cover), imps and monsters, which, as Monkhouse points out, reveal a Gothic imagination on a par with Lewis Carroll's, and which were fostered by Martin's work on the Gothic carvings of the new Houses of Parliament (figures 26 and 27). The shapes of Martin-ware were derived from many sources apart from fantasy; in particular the brothers studied examples of prehistoric pottery and Romano-British glassware in the British Museum. The last phase of the Martins' work is described in a later section.

IV Vase, earthenware. Doulton Faience (Doulton and Co.), decorated by M.M. Arding. Height 7¾ins. Dated 1879.

Painted Pottery of the Aesthetic Movement

In the late 1860s, the art of faience painting was revived in Europe at the studio of Théodore Deck in Paris. To paint his ware, Deck employed Salon artists, and at the Paris World Exhibition of 1867 he showed circular plaques painted by Eléonore Escallier-Légerot, a pupil of J. C. Ziegler, and Félix Bracquemond, a prominent graphic artist who had previously decorated, in the style of Hokusai drawings, a dinner-service modelled by Eugène Rousseau. A plaque by Eléonore Escallier-Légerot was purchased from the exhibition for the South Kensington Museum.

Deck's faience was almost certainly the spur to William S. Coleman when, as G.W. Rhead wrote (quoted on p.56), he applied to Copeland's and then to Minton's for china-painting facilities. It is significant that it was Minton's and not Copeland's who obliged; it must have weighed heavily on Minton that Wedgwood's had achieved considerable success at the international exhibitions at London in 1862 and Paris in 1867 with their pottery painted by Emile Lessore, who had spent a few months in 1858 at Minton's before moving to Etruria. Lessore had been a pupil of Ingres and an exhibitor at the Paris Salon before he started painting ceramics at the Sèvres factory. From the mid-1860s, Minton's had employed another Continental painter, Edouard Rischgitz, whose style, like Lessore's was broader and more painterly than that conventionally used by china-painters.

Rhead's description of the establishment, the progress, and the disastrous end of Minton's Art Pottery Studio in Kensington Gore, London (figures 28 - 31), is very full. It pinpoints a dilemma which continued to occupy artists and critics throughout what Rhead called the 'craze' for painting on pottery: whether a piece of painted pottery should emulate a picture, or should be designed with more regard to the material and given a broad decorative treatment. The contrast is illustrated in figures 35 and 36. Writers on the subject generally concurred that the flatness and hardness of the china should be recognised, and that the perspective and chiaroscuro which were still considered *de rigueur* for oil-painting should be avoided.

On the other hand, Sparkes in his comments on Doulton Faience (figures 32 - 36 and colour plates IV and V) and Impasto (figures 37 and 38) wares (quoted on p.44) made the point that the latter technique enabled the artist to achieve effects of surface texture and light which were otherwise to be found only in tempera- or oil-painting. The Impasto technique involved the application of thin coloured slips, rather than flat transparent colours. It was introduced from France, where it was known as *barbotine* (from the clay shavings which were used for the coloured slips) and had been developed in 1871 by Ernest Chaplet working for Laurin at Bourg-la-Reine.

Doulton's began producing Faience in 1872. The ware is readily distinguishable from the work of Minton's Art Pottery Studio because of the brown earthenware body which gives a warm golden tone to the colours. The pictorial areas were often bounded by pattern in a manner reminiscent of Japanese ornament. Some pieces were painted overall with ornament inspired by Persian or sixteenth-century Italian originals (figure 33). In 1878 Doulton bought the Pinder, Bourne and Co. works at Burslem, where blanks were made for painting at Lambeth (figure 36). Most of the artists who painted on Doulton Faience were recruited from the Lambeth School of Art.

Howell and James, a firm of a china retailers in London, soon filled the gap left by the destruction of Minton's Art Pottery Studio. They commissioned Staffordshire potteries to supply biscuit blanks which, like the special ceramic colours manufactured by Hancock and

V   Plaque, earthenware. Doulton Faience (Doulton and Co.). Diameter 12¼ins. Circa 1880.

Sons of Worcester, were available from their Lower Regent Street store (figures 39 - 42). The firing of the painted pottery was also arranged by Howell and James. The instruction which students had had from professional artists and ceramists at Kensington Gore, Howell and James could not replace, although they did publish a handbook prepared by J. Sparkes and the Derby porcelain-painter John Haslem. Several other handbooks appeared during the late 1870s and early '80s.

To give impetus to the venture, Howell and James organised annual competitive exhibitions of paintings on china from 1876. These events were patronised by royalty who provided many of the prizes, and were judged by distinguished Royal Academicians. Competition was divided into two main classes, professional and amateur, the number in the latter category growing steadily each year until a decline became apparent and the exhibitions were discontinued in the mid-1880s. Similar competitions were organised in provincial centres, and Howell and James arranged a special exhibit of amateur work at the Paris Fair of 1878, in which the two plaques painted by Edith Cowper illustrated as figures 41 and 42 were included.

The names of several artists appear regularly in the lists of prize-winners. Portraits of her children by the Viscountess Hood won for her at least two of the Crown Princess of Germany's Gold Medals. Miss Everett Green's flower-studies were also successful on more than one occasion. Most of the professional competitors were from the ranks of the artists decorating Lambeth Faience: Florence Lewis, Linnie Watt, Hannah Barlow, Charlotte Spiers, Ellen Welby, Ada Hanbury, Edith Hall and Mrs. Sparkes were all commended by the critics. Two interesting names which appear among the competitors are Lewis F. Day, who subsequently designed for Maw and Co. and Pilkington's, and Camille Moreau (later Moreau-Nélaton), a French lady who used the clay of Bourg-la-Reine and had her work fired by Laurin.

The period of greatest enthusiasm for painted pottery coincided with the years of the most rampant Aestheticism. Charles Eastlake, in his *Hints on Household Taste* (1868) attacked the products of the various house-furnishing industries as being designed without regard to basic principles of which anyone would be aware who had made the shallowest study of the great historical styles. In his chapter on 'Crockery' he referred the reader to the achievements of the Italian *maiolica* painters, and in a footnote to a later edition he wrote: 'Mr. W. S. Coleman, in his figure-subject designs for modern ware, manufactured by Messrs. Minton & Co. at their art pottery works, has realised much of the true spirit of old majolica'. In the context of Coleman's work (figure 28) reference to Italian *maiolica* seems strange, but Eastlake's point, presumably, is that his treatment is flat and decorative, a treatment that Coleman, however, derived from Japanese prints. A more direct reference to early *maiolica*, by an unidentified artist, is illustrated in figure 29.

The decoration of the Green Dining Room at the South Kensington Museum by Morris and Co. in 1866, and of the museum's Grill Room by Edward Poynter and the ladies of the National Art Training School in 1868, were practical demonstrations that greater effects could be achieved by simpler means. It was realised that enthusiastic amateurs guided by artists could create the beautiful more surely than could the pundits of the decorating trade, who claimed to purvey it at so many shillings per yard. From Minton's Art Pottery Studio, a writer in the *Art Journal* of 1872 hoped 'to see the springing up of a really national school of painters in pottery, untrammelled by the mere conventionalities and trade traditions of the past.'

The frustration felt by women in an age of exclusive masculinism contributed to the vogue for art-work which characterised the Aesthetic Movement. Embroidery and painting on pottery were two crafts which could be carried on at home without incommoding the household, and which provided the opportunity to display the sketching skills which ladies were expected to acquire in the course of their education. Much contemporary comment on pottery-painting emphasises its function of occupying otherwise idle women, and of providing them with a means of livelihood if necessary.

One effect of the vogue for pottery-painting was that it gave outsiders further knowledge of, and access to, ceramic processes. At about the same time as Edwin and Walter Martin were learning pottery techniques at Doulton's works in Lambeth, William De Morgan was, according to Rhead, benefiting from the amenities offered by Minton's in Kensington Gore.

Wedgwood's produced some pottery decorated with coloured slip, similar in technique to *barbotine*. The designs usually incorporated motifs from Japanese and Gothic ornament (figure 43 and colour plate VI), but were sometimes abstract (figure 44). Other art potteries responded to the fashion by producing painted wares in addition to their normal lines (figures 45 and 46).

Pre-Raphaelite Pottery

The term 'Pre-Raphaelite' to define the pottery produced by William De Morgan and Harold Rathbone is by way of being a *pis aller*. There are grounds for grouping together the two enterprises, and 'Pre-Raphaelite' may be defended as the epithet most applicable to their homogeneity.

The painters of the Pre-Raphaelite Brotherhood abandoned their corporate identity almost as soon as they had assumed it. Subsequent efforts to revive a spirit of communal activity, such as attended the decoration of the Oxford Union and the exhibitions of the Hogarth Club, had been unavailing, but in 1861 Ford Madox Brown, D. G. Rossetti and Edward Burne-Jones were among the founding members of Morris, Marshall, Faulkner and Co., Fine Art Workmen. The workshops of 'the Firm' as the new enterprise was known were in Red Lion Square, London.

On leaving the Royal Academy Schools, where he had been weaned of any ambition to be a painter, William De Morgan became associated with the Fine Art Workmen of Red Lion Square. In the paper he read to the Society of Arts in 1892 (reprinted in part on p.73) he tells how his work on stained glass led directly to his interest in lustre decoration. Probably it was at the time of his family moving from Fitzroy Square, where, as he says, he had burnt the roof off, to Chelsea, in 1872, that he availed himself of the facilities afforded by Minton's Art Pottery Studio.

De Morgan's paper and Reginald Blunt's narrative (quoted on p.67) provide a full description of the pottery, but a little may be added regarding his achievement as an artist-potter. His father was a distinguished mathematician and De Morgan obviously took great delight in the application of logic and a little ingenuity to the solution of technical problems as they confronted him. However, for many years his designs were executed on blanks bought from the industry. As a ceramist his achievement lies primarily in the development of copper, silver and gold lustres (figures 47 - 51 and colour plate VII), and in his reproduction of the colours used in the decoration of Persian pottery (figures 52 - 60). He trained himself to be an accomplished ceramic chemist.

De Morgan is perhaps to be most highly regarded as an artist and designer. To the Pre-Raphaelites, as their name implies, the malign effect of the Italian High Renaissance on the course of European art was an article of faith, and it was natural that De Morgan should turn to the wares of the Middle Ages and Persia for inspiration. However, his appreciation of past styles was catholic; in 1892, from Florence, he wrote to Halsey Ricardo: 'I hope to find when I come back a mine of pots that might be Greek, Sicilian, Etruscan, Moorish, Italian Renaissance - anything but Staffordshire.' Eastlake, in *Hints on Household Taste* (1868) illustrated and described a 'Moorish plate'. He wrote: 'The whole thing is, pictorially considered, absolute nonsense, and yet, as a bit of decorative painting excellent.' This remark might equally refer to most examples of De Morgan's work.

The style developed by De Morgan was personal, despite its antecedents in Persian and Hispano-Moresque pottery. It is a style which is related to that of William Morris, for both conceived their designs as two-dimensional patterns. But the work of each is readily distinguishable. De Morgan often shows a feeling for the grotesque which is generally absent in Morris' work, while Morris' almost idolatrous respect for naturalistic detail in his rendering of flowers and fruits is seldom to be found in the more mythological creations, animal and vegetable, of De Morgan.

Most of the decoration of his pottery was designed by De Morgan himself. William Morris did three deigns for tiles, and Dr. Reginald Thompson is said to have done some of the early designs of animals. The 'Orpheus' dish, quite uncharacteristic of De Morgan ware, was designed by Edward Burne-Jones. Some relief tiles made in the later years of the pottery were designed by Halsey Ricardo.

In the late 1870s two Shropshire potteries, Maw and Co. and Craven Dunnill started to produce lustre- and Persian- decorated wares in a manner close to De Morgan's work (figures 61 - 66). (De Morgan refers in his paper to 'employés' who took the knowledge of his methods elsewhere). These firms made large quantities of tiles decorated in a style analogous to De Morgan's, but hollow ware was also made, notably some pieces designed by Walter Crane (figures 61 and 62). Crane was a well-known artist and designer, a close friend of Morris and Burne-Jones, whose style was chiefly derived from the Italian masters of the *quattrocento*. Lewis F. Day also designed for Maw's. James Pearson claimed to have decorated in De Morgan's studio, and he subsequently painted commercial blanks with designs in the style of, but vastly inferior to, De Morgan (figure 67). He used silver and gold lustre, usually with green, blue and black.

The Della Robbia Pottery Co. was founded at Birkenhead in 1893 by Harold Rathbone and the sculptor Conrad Dressler. Although the primary purpose was to make architectural faience, a wide variety of hollow ware was also produced from the outset (figures 68 - 80 and colour plate VIII). Like De Morgan, Rathbone had close connections with Morris and the Pre-Raphaelite movement: Holman Hunt was a member of a controlling council which was formed at the firm's foundation, and Rathbone had been a pupil of Ford Madox Brown. The company executed pottery panels of *King Alfred* (figure 75), *Elkana, Isaac* and *The Young Milton* after original drawings by Brown; other panels were based on designs by Edward Burne-Jones.

The organisation of the firm was not unlike that of De Morgan's, with Rathbone supervising a group of artists and technicians working in studio conditions. On the other hand, the artists of the Della Robbia Pottery, who were mostly recruited from local art-schools, were encouraged to develop their own individual styles and to originate their own designs. Carlo Manzoni, who had run his own pottery at Hanley, joined the company and probably provided most of the technical expertise. The quality of manufacture was generally low, many pieces being cracked in firing. But the imperfections emphasise the high regard in which decorative success was held by Rathbone; technical quality was not a matter of importance, provided the piece was artistic. Ruskin's precepts were well taken at Birkenhead.

The decorative technique used was usually *sgraffito*. The reddish biscuit ware was coated in white slip, through which the decorative design was incised. Colour was then applied to the design. This was the manner of decoration used by the makers of *mezza-maiolica* in fifteenth-century Italy, and many of the forms were inspired by Renaissance originals. The architectural wares were coloured, and much of it has a close stylistic resemblance to the Della Robbia's work. Some of the hollow ware was decorated in a manner reminiscent of Middle Eastern pottery. However, the predominant style of decoration was an English version of Art Nouveau, which consists primarily of stylised floral motifs grouped in formal arrangements. It was the art-school style of the time and is to be found in profusion in the pages of *The Studio,* which was published from 1893.

Among the artists who designed for the Della Robbia Pottery Co. were E. M. Rope (figure 78) and R. Anning Bell, the director of the Liverpool School of Art and Architecture, whose work was frequently illustrated in *The Studio.* In 1895 Conrad Dressler (figure 81) set up a pottery on his own, the Medmenham Pottery at Marlow, Buckinghamshire, where he produced ceramic sculpture and pictorial panels.

VI   Vase, earthenware. J. Wedgwood & Sons. Height 7ins. Circa 1880.

The Della Robbia Pottery Co. was never a successful commercial venture, although Sarah Bernhardt and Paderewski were among their patrons. In 1900, it amalgamated with a Liverpool firm of ecclesiastical sculptors under the title of The Della Robbia Pottery and Marble Co. Ltd., but still did not prosper. In 1906 the pottery was closed. The following year saw the closure of De Morgan's works at Fulham, although Frank Iles and the Passenger brothers continued working in the Brompton Road until 1911. Fred Passenger painted pottery and tiles at Bushey Heath between 1921 and 1933.

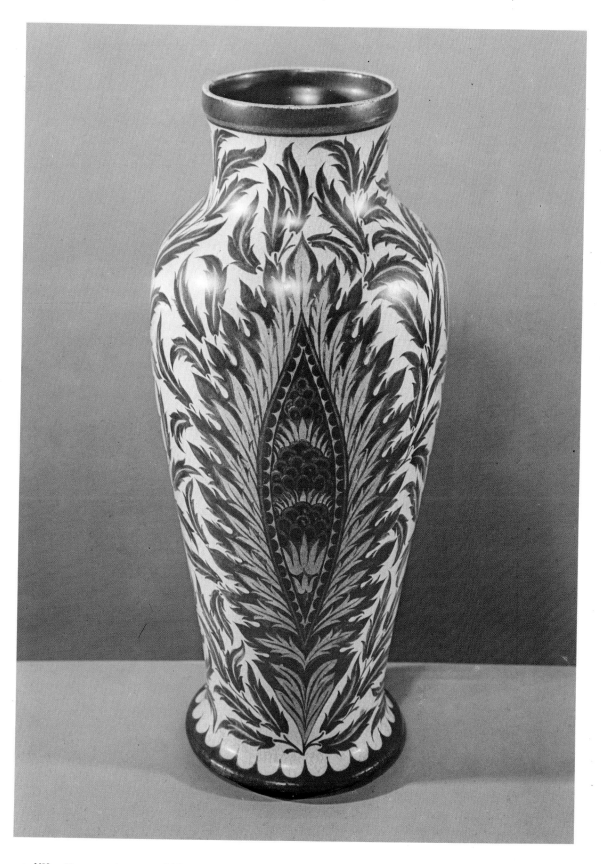

VII   Vase, earthenware. William De Morgan, decorated by James Hersey. Height 13½ins. Circa 1895.

Art Pottery from the West Country

Geology has made the West Country a natural location for potters. The fine clays found in Somerset and Devon have been exploited for centuries, and still attract discerning ceramists today. But until the art-pottery movement of the later nineteenth century, the work produced there was generally functional ware of a rustic nature, without any but the humblest artistic pretension.

Terracotta was a popular material during much of the Victorian era. In the 1840s and '50s a taste for the Classical had brought a rash of terracotta ware on to the market. At the Great Exhibition of 1851 it was featured among the displays of many leading firms. Minton's, Copeland's, and F. & R. Pratt produced it in quantity, and in the Paris Exhibition of 1867 it was shown by Doulton's alongside their stoneware. A terracotta fountain, designed by John Sparkes, was exhibited by Doulton's at South Kensington in 1871. At the same exhibition the products of the Watcombe Terra-cotta Co. were first shown to the public, and they were received with enthusiasm.

The work of the pottery at Watcombe (figs. 46, 82-87, and colour plate IX), founded in 1867, is reviewed by Professor Archer in a notice which appeared in the *Art Journal* in 1878 (reprinted on p.81). The early wares produced would hardly qualify as art pottery but for the fact that the promoters' aims were so thoroughly in accord with the teaching of John Ruskin. But the simple forms and geometric decoration, of both the earlier examples in the Classical style (figs. 82 and 83) and the later wares inspired by Japanese ceramics (fig. 84 and colour plate IX), suggest that G.J. Allen and Charles Brock were aware from the outset of the more advanced theories of design. It has been suggested that designs for some Watcombe pieces were supplied by Dr. Christopher Dresser, who had taught at the School of Design in London and had contributed to Owen Jones's *Grammar of Ornament* an illustration which shows how plant forms might be adapted as geometric motifs.

The Torquay Terra-cotta Co. Ltd. produced wares in a style emulous of the Watcombe firm between 1875 and 1909 (fig. 88). The pottery produced at Watcombe became more varied, many different types of decorative technique being employed (figs. 85 to 87), and in 1901 it merged with the nearby Aller Vale Art Potteries (fig. 89) to become the Royal Aller Vale & Watcombe Pottery Co. John Phillips had started the Aller Vale Art Potteries in 1881; the wares produced were quaintly rustic in form and decorated by local art students.

One of the decorative techniques used at Watcombe was *sgraffito*. Its popularity had been promoted by the Barum Ware made by Charles Brannam at Barnstaple (figs. 90-98). This town, at the other end of Devon from Watcombe, had for some time been a pottery centre which produced architectural wares and flower-pots in terracotta as well as keeping the local inhabitants supplied with slip-decorated utensils.

Charles Brannam, whose father owned two potteries in Barnstaple, showed an early artistic talent. At fifteen he won the Queen's Prize for Chalk Drawing. He became a student at the Barnstaple School of Art, the headmaster of which was Alexander Lauder. Another distinguished pupil of Lauder's at Barnstaple was W.R. Lethaby, a noted designer of the Arts and Crafts movement who became principle of the Central School of Art in London. In 1876 Lauder set up his own pottery in Barnstaple and started producing artistic wares (figs. 99 and 100). This probably inspired Brannam to try the same line when he rented one of his father's potteries in 1879. At about the same time, O.W. Davis (in the article from *The Artist* of 1881 reprinted on p.83 his initials are wrongly given), a well-known designer of ornament, was in Barnstaple. He made some pottery himself, examples of which have been found, dated 1879 and 1881. It is not clear from the article in *The Artist* exactly what his position was *vis à vis* Bannam's pottery, but he may well have been instrumental in drawing it to the attention of Professor Church and 'one of the partners of the well-known firm of Messrs. Howell and James' (mentioned by Cosmo Monkhouse in his article on Brannam reprinted on p.48), who was, in fact, Mr. James.

The Barum Ware produced during the 1880s is decorated in a style which is close to that of O. W. Davis as it appears in his *Art and Work* (1885), an illustrated treatise on decorative art. Apart from Brannam there were two artists making Barum Ware at this time, James Dewdney (figures 91, 94, 95, 97) and William Leonard Baron, although it is not clear whether they threw their own vessels or were merely decorators. Baron left Brannam's pottery in 1893 and subsequently started his own at Rolle Quay, Barnstaple. Dewdney continued to work for Brannam until well into the twentieth century. His decoration, like that of Barum Ware in general, becomes looser in the 1890s, more of the design being applied in slip and less incised through it. This less painstaking process may have resulted from pressure of demand. In the late 1890s grotesque birds and animals were made to designs by F. Carruthers Gould; and in the early twentieth century, when Brannam was making pottery for Liberty's, a great deal of the decoration was in the Celtic Art Nouveau style.

The accounts of Edmund Elton's pottery (figures 101 - 103) given by Cosmo Monkhouse in 1882 (reprinted on p.84), and by the potter himself in 1910 (reprinted on p.92) to some extent overlap. But comparison between the two is of interest, partly because one is written by the critic and connoisseur and the other by the artist-potter, and partly because they were written nearly thirty years apart. Elton was a complete artist-potter; starting without any knowledge of ceramics, he picked up technical information and assistance wherever he could until he was able himself to perform all the tasks involved in the manufacture and decoration of his pottery. His work, both the slipware and the lustreware, reveal him as a man of artistic sensibility. It is only regrettable that he was inhibited by a lack of technical competence from attempting a more varied *œuvre*.

VIII   Plate, earthenware. Della Robbia Pottery, decorated by Annie Smith. Diameter 9ins. Dated 1895.

IX   Teapot, earthenware. Watcombe Pottery Co. Height 4½ins. Circa 1880.

Form and Colour

The art pottery described so far implied fundamental changes in the attitudes of both producers and consumers to the manufacture of ceramic works of art. The production of technical *tours de force* in a variety of revival styles, and their cheap imitations, had dominated Victorian ceramics until *circa* 1870; it remained, and remains today, an important aspect of an elaborate industrial and commercial organisation. But during the early years of the art-pottery movement, the philosophy had been preached, and practised, that pottery as art would better be produced if individual talent were given greater artistic freedom than conditions in the industry generally allowed, and encouraged to develop the decorative potential of the ceramic medium. The pottery described in this section was produced in such a theoretical climate, but is further characterised by a desire to extend considerably the aesthetic frontiers of modern ceramics beyond the current concepts of form and decoration.

The Linthorpe Art Pottery was founded in 1879 (figures 45, 104 - 109 and colour plate X). It was situated in Linthorpe, a village near Middlesbrough, where there already existed the Sun Brick Works. The owner of the land which included the site of the brick works, John Harrison, met Dr. Christopher Dresser, an architect and ornamentalist. Dresser's previous connections with pottery seem to have been limited to providing designs for the artists at Minton's Art Pottery Studio in Kensington Gore, London. He had visited Japan (1876 - 77) and in his account of its architecture and decorative arts, published in 1882, described the ceramics produced there. Dresser suggested to Harrison that part of the brick works should be given over to the production of art-pottery, using the same local clay as was used for the bricks. Harrison concurred, and results from the first firing, which was supervised by the kiln-manager from the Stockton Pottery, were sufficiently encouraging to proceed with the equipping of decorating studios and the recruitment of staff.

Dresser was made Art Superintendent and called in the decorative artist Henry Tooth as pottery manager. Tooth came north from Ryde in the Isle of Wight, visiting Staffordshire *en route* to gain a basic knowledge of pottery production, and, no doubt, to recruit some experienced technicians. A thrower from a pottery in Middlesbrough was engaged, and fourteen decorators were recruited from the students of the South Kensington art school.

The decoration of Linthorpe ware was executed in a variety of techniques including *sgraffito,* impasto, painted and incised ornament. The designs were mostly of birds and flowers in the Japanese manner, and contemporary photographs of the decorating studios show the walls hung with Japanese prints and silk pictures. In 1879, Dresser in partnership with Charles Holme set up a business importing Japanese and other oriental wares, which were sold at show-rooms in Faringdon Road, London.

As is evident from the *Notes on Linthorpe Ware* (reprinted on p.95), the artistic direction taken by Dresser and Tooth was towards an emphasis on form and glazes. This had not been the principal preoccupation of any ceramicist in England previously. Léon Arnoux, at Minton's, had made a number of experiments with glaze effects in emulation of Chinese originals, as had Théodore Deck in France, and, during the 1880s, Ernest Chaplet in Paris, Hermann Seger in Berlin and Clement in Copenhagen all experimented with *flambé* glazes. At Linthorpe, the significance of decoration with glaze effects was not technical, but aesthetic. At first, using brick clay and glazes bought from manufacturers in Staffordshire, the firing temperature of Linthorpe ware must have been low and the possibilities limited. Subsequently, Cornish clays were introduced and the glazes were ground and mixed at Linthorpe under the direction of H. Venables, a Staffordshire potter. Firing temperatures were still no higher than about 1200°C, but a considerable range of glaze colours were achieved.

The *Notes* suggest that the aesthetics of decoration with coloured glazes were inspired by Oriental pottery. The emphasis on pure form, however, was derived from principles of European artistic theory which had been gathering strength since they were promulgated by Goethe at the beginning of the nineteenth century. The basic idea behind Dresser's thinking was that form should be allowed to speak for itself; that ornament should be subservient to form, or even absent from it altogether, so that the intellectual qualities of shape and proportion could be seen to greater advantage. In this respect, Dresser was a revolutionary, and Linthorpe ware a precursor of twentieth-century studio ceramics.

Methods of production, however, were more conventional. The ware was cast in plaster of paris moulds and the decorative processes carried out by different artists according to their skills. One technical innovation was the use of gas-fired kilns. It was always part of Dresser's philosophy to make full use of industrial techniques which lowered the cost of an object without reducing its aesthetic merit. In this respect, he stands as a follower of Josiah Wedgwood rather than a forerunner of Bernard Leach.

Gradually, Christopher Dresser's connection with the Linthorpe Art Pottery weakened, and he stopped designing for it in 1882. Many examples of Linthorpe ware are impressed with his facsimile signature indicating that he designed the shape. Henry Tooth also left Linthorpe in 1882 and his place was taken by Richard Patey, who had come with Tooth from the Isle of Wight. At the height of its success, Linthorpe ware was shown at an exhibition of modern pottery arranged by the Society of Arts in London, 1882, alongside Worcester, Wedgwood, Minton and Doulton. But by 1890 the pottery had closed. The rising price of Cornish clay, John Harrison's bankruptcy, and the decline of popular interest in advanced art which had characterised the Aesthetic Movement, combined to bring the enterprise to an end.

The story of Burmantofts Faience (figures 110 - 123) is much the same as that of Linthorpe ware. Wilcock and Co. were manufacturing fire-brick and drainpipes at Leeds until 1880 when production of architectural faience began, quickly followed by art-pottery. Methods of production and decoration closely paralleled those of Linthorpe, though the import of Continental artists such as V. Kremer (not Kreimer as given in the article from *The Artist* reprinted on p.98) and B. Sicard, gave some pieces a more exotic look. Kremer's modelling (figures 114 - 117) reflects the Palissy revival, and Sicard worked in a manner suggesting the *barbotine* artists of France. Production of Burmantofts Faience survived the take-over, in 1904, of Wilcock's by the Leeds Fire-Clay Co. Ltd.; the name of this firm is impressed on later examples, which include pieces decorated in lustre (figures 120 - 123). Burmantofts faience was also decorated in a manner derived from the work of William De Morgan (figure 119).

In 1883, the year after he had left Linthorpe, Henry Tooth set up his own firm in partnership with William Ault at Woodville, near Burton-on-Trent. The ware produced was called Bretby Art Pottery (figs. 124-131) and in most respects was similar to Linthorpe ware, although many of the designs, which emulated Dresser's in sophistication of form, are weak. Wares simulating metalwork, in an Art Nouveau style, were produced in quantity around the turn of the century (figs. 129-131). Usually the quality of Bretby pottery is low, and by the early twentieth century, when Clantha ware was manufactured, standards had dropped to such a level that the product was indistinguishable from the cheapest decorative pottery made in Staffordshire.

William Ault left Tooth in 1887 and established his own works at Swadlincote. Ault ware (figs. 132-136) was generally unremarkable, but in the later 1890s designs were provided by Christopher Dresser. Many pieces were painted by William Ault's daughter in a loose sketchy style which works well on a small scale (fig. 136).

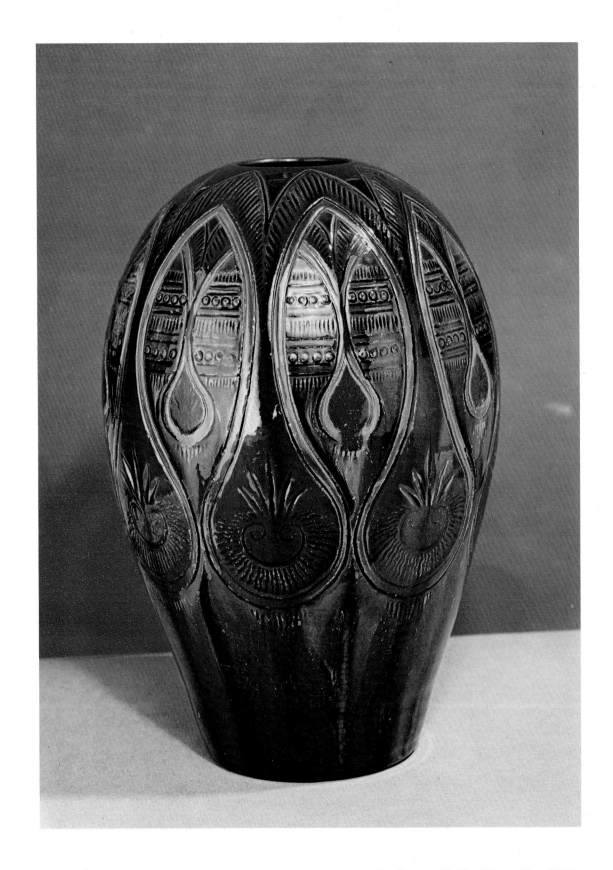

X Vase, earthenware. Linthorpe Pottery, designed by Christopher Dresser. Height 9¼ins. Circa 1880.

XI   Charger, earthenware. Pilkington's Tile and Pottery Co., designed by Walter Crane, decorated by C.E. Cundall. Diameter 19ins. Dated 1912.

From Art Pottery to Studio Pottery

By 1900, art pottery, known in the retail trade as 'novelty wares', was being produced in a wide variety of techniques, styles and quality. But the Aesthetic Movement had ended, its obsequies performed at Oscar Wilde's final trial, and the Arts and Crafts Movement supporters favoured a more austere style than had prevailed in the '70s and '80s. They abhorred *l'Art Nouveau*, which was well represented at the 1900 Paris Exhibition and was gaining popularity in Britain. A writer in the *Magazine of Art* of 1899 suggested: 'There has been of late years such a large production of so-called "art pottery" that [it] has almost become a term of reproach, whether regarded from the point of view of design or decoration'.

This observation, however, prefaces a laudatory notice of the 'Florian' ware produced by James Macintyre and Co. at Burslem under the artistic direction of William Moorcroft (figs. 137-142). The ware, mostly in classical forms, was decorated with floral designs in an *art nouveau* style, the linear designs being applied in slip and the spaces being coloured with metallic oxides. The technique was a refinement of tube-lining, where outlines in slip were trailed on to the surface by means of a tubular tool, on the same principle as decorating a cake with icing. Tube-lining became a popular form of decoration in the Potteries at this time, particularly for tiles. Minton's produced art pottery decorated in this way, sometimes to designs by Léon Solon and J.W. Wadsworth.

At Macintyre's works, Moorcroft formed a group of decorators, mostly women, who had been trained at the Burslem Art School. For Liberty's, the Regent Street, London store, which retailed many Macintyre lines, Moorcroft designed 'Flamminian' ware, often in more outlandish shapes and decorated with more abstract *art nouveau* motifs (fig. 142). In 1913, he left Macintyres and set up his own works at Cobridge, on the outskirts of Burslem, taking with him many of his decorators and craftsmen, as well as the moulds.

Other decorated pottery which continued to be produced in the Edwardian era were the De Morgan and Della Robbia wares, described above. The style of their decoration, which derived from Pre-Raphaelite sources, was again adopted for the lustreware produced by Pilkington's from 1903 (figs. 143-154 and colour plate X1). Ten years before, William Burton had been appointed manager of the Pilkington Tile and Pottery Co. at Clifton Junction, near Manchester. He had previously worked as a chemist for Wedgwood's and combined considerable knowledge of ceramic technology with great artistic sensibility. Already he had commissioned tile designs from Lewis F. Day and the architect C.F.A. Voysey, and when the production of lustreware began he selected a number of talented artists to design and execute the decoration. Among them were Richard Joyce who specialised in animals and fishes, Gordon Forsyth, whose lettering and heraldic designs are notable, Charles Cundall and William Mycock. Some designs were commissioned from Walter Crane (colour plate X1). The motifs of animals, flowers, galleons etc. are in the same Hispano-Moresque and Italian *maiolica* tradition as William De Morgan's lustreware designs.

Alfred Powell and hs wife Louise painted pottery for Wedgwood's from about 1905. The Powells were closely connected to leading figures of the Arts and Crafts Movement, such as Ernest Gimson and the Barnsley brothers; Alfred Powell frequently carried out painted scenes on the furniture they produced. The paintings they did on Wedgwood pottery were sometimes pastoral scenes (often actual landscapes) and they were usually within borders of scrolling leaves or flowers; on many pieces bands of flowers or leaves extended over the whole area. Floral and abstract designs were also painted in lustres. The Powells had their own pottery where they made simply shaped vases, bowls and jugs decorated with lustres (fig. 155). They experimented successfully with painting on tin glaze. The type of decoration which the Powells introduced at Wedgwood's was also executed by a number of factory artists whom they trained.

Painted china was made at the Doulton factoy in Burslem from about 1884, but it was mostly close in style to the traditional Staffordshire product. In 1895 Holbein ware was introduced, and in 1898 Rembrandt ware, on which, as the name implies, surface effects added to the vitality of the painting; these lines came in simple moulded shapes and were painted with landscapes, figures and heads. China figures were also produced at Doulton's Burslem factory during the Edwardian era; models were commissioned from Charles Vyse and Phoebe Stabler, young sculptors who both subsequently set up their own potteries (fig.156).

There were more significant developments at Burslem. In the course of the 1890s, John Slater, the art director, and Charles Noke, who had previously worked for the Royal Worcester Porcelain Co., began making experiments with the aim of emulating the *rouge flambé* and *sang-de-boeuf* glaze effects on Chinese ceramics (figs. 157-159). These effects are known as 'transmutation' glazes and require very precise control over atmospheric conditions inside the kiln. The efforts of Henry Tooth and William Ault, described in the previous section, to rival Oriental glaze effects had always been thwarted by technical problems, such as kilns which provided insufficient heat and control, and bodies which would not stand up to the high temperature firings necessary.

Apart from Noke and Slater of Doulton's, who were joined in their experiments in 1901 by Cuthbert Bailey, the son of the works-manager, other ceramists were trying to achieve oriental glaze effects at about the same time. The possibilities had been revealed to them not only by the Linthorpe enterprise, but also by greater achievements abroad: Chaplet, Delaherche and Dalpayrat in France, Seger and Mutz in Germany, Engelhardt in Denmark. Improved technology provided the means, and the aesthetic trend away from decorated pottery spurred the experimenters' zeal.

In 1905, the Moore Brothers porcelain works at Longton was sold up, and Bernard Moore started his own enterprise in Stoke (figs. 160-163 and colour plates XII and XIII). For several years, in association with Cuthbert Bailey, he had been experimenting with *flambé* glazes, sometimes using Chinese blanks specially imported. Moore also made decorative *flambé* ware (colour plate XII), employing a group of artists which included Hilda Beardmore, Dora Billington and John Adams; sometimes their designs were heightened with gilding and turquoise blue enamelling. Two of Moore's pupils manufactured *flambé* ware under their own names, E.R. Wilkes and J. Howson (fig.164). At Doulton's *flambé* china was also painted, usually with landscapes but sometimes with more fanciful designs of animals or goblins etc. Charles Noke also experimented with crystalline glaze effects, usually in white, but these were found too expensive to produce and were discontinued. At G.L. Ashworth & Bros. of Hanley, the firm who in 1862 had bought the rights to the patent of Mason's Ironstone china, J.V. Goddard started making *flambé* glazed ceramics at about the same time (fig. 165). It is noticeable that, like the Doulton experiments, these ventures were undertaken in connection with the production of china or porcelain, where the ceramists could benefit from long experience of firing at high temperatures.

A remarkable achievement was that of William Howson Taylor, the son of the headmaster of the Birmingham Art School; in 1898, after working briefly at Howson's he built his own pottery at West Smethwick and with the help of some craftsmen from Wedgwood's, he began experimenting with high-temperature glazes (figs. 166-173 and colour plate XIV). He called his enterprise the Ruskin Pottery. Eventually, he achieved a remarkable range of high-temperature glaze effects, as well as lustres (fig. 174) and monochromes (which he called

XII   Pot-pourri jar and cover, porcelain. Bernard Moore. Height 8¾ins. Circa 1910.

XIII   Vase, porcelain. Bernard Moore. Height 5½ins. Circa 1910.

'soufflé' glazes) (fig. 175). In 1904, his *flambé* ware won him a Grand Prix at the St. Louis Centennial Exhibition.

Another enterprise was the Ashby Potters' Guild established by Pascoe Tunnicliffe at Woodville, Derbyshire, in 1909 (fig. 176 and colour plate XV). Tunnicliffe came from a family of potters. The Guild, which specialised in glaze effects, was merged with Ault's in 1922 as Ault and Tunnicliffe.

At Poole, in Dorset, Owen Carter, son of the owner of Carter & Co. and a friend of William de Morgan, to whom his father's firm had supplied tile-blanks, successfully experimented with lustre glazes (fig. 177). Pieces, often signed by Carter himself, were produced up to the outbreak of the Great War, when the firm began making a ware, covered in white slip and painted with simple designs in bold colours, which made Poole Pottery famous in the 1920s and '30s (fig. 178-180). The simple decoration and primitive forms (fig. 178) of this ware suggest the aesthetic influence of Roger Fry, who went to the factory at Poole (*circa* 1912) to learn pottery. He subsequently made ceramics at the Omega Workshops.

Before their painted lustreware, described above, Pilkington's had experimented with several glaze effects, including *flambé*, aventurine (fig. 181) and monochromes (figs. 182-184); they continued to produce the wares alongside the lustreware. At Benthall, near Broseley, in Shropshire, the Salopian Art Pottery Co. also produced vases with glaze effects (figs. 185-186). In accordance with the trend towards abstract decoration of art pottery, both Edmund Elton and the Martin Brothers started making this type of ware. The experiments leading to the production of Elton's lustreware (figs. 188-193) are described by the potter himself in the article reprinted on p.92. The incised, inlaid and modelled ware made by the Martins from the late 1890s (described in the article from *The Studio* of 1908 reprinted on p.104) was considered by contemporary Martinware collectors to be perhaps their greatest achievement (figs. 194-199). Robert Wallace Martin continued to make tobacco-jars in the shape of grotesque birds, and jugs with comic masks. Walter Martin died in 1912, and Edwin in 1915, a few months after the last firing. At Doulton's Lambeth factory, gourd-vases related to the Martins' work were produced in the early years of the twentieth century; F.C. Pope was the artist mainly involved.

Referring to the new opportunities provided by tuition in practical pottery at art schools, H.M. Pemberton, in 1911, wrote: 'It is now quite within the bounds of the possible for many an artist or person of artistic taste and ability to have each his own little pottery in his garden....' (*Art Journal*, 1911, p. 123). Among the earliest to avail themselves of these opportunities were William Staite Murray (at Camberwell School of Art) and Denise Wren (at Kingston). But their work really belongs to the years after the Great War. Reginald Wells, however, turned from sculpture to pottery in about 1909, working first at Wrotham in Kent, and from 1910 at Chelsea. His first pottery was brown earthenware decorated with white slip, in the style of the seventeenth-century English ware, but he also made ceramic sculpture and experimented with high-temperature glaze effects (figs. 200 and 201).

George Cox, the author of *Pottery for Artists, Craftsmen and Teachers*, started his studio-pottery at Mortlake in about 1911. His wares are often decorated with modelling or incised designs, and he too experimented with high-temperature glaze effects (figs. 202, 203 and colour plate XVI). S. Wakeley started the Upchurch Pottery at Rainham, Kent, in 1913, which produced matt-glazed wares in soft colours (figs. 204 and 205); many pieces were designed by Edward Spencer, who also designed metalwork for the Artificers' Guild.

These artists exemplify the emancipation of the craft of pottery from the industrial situation to which it had for so long been restricted. In the article already quoted, H.M. Pemberton claimed: 'Now, in this as in other artistic crafts, the Pandora's box of treasures is opened, and secrets for so long carefully guarded by "the trade" are exposed for those who care to avail themselves of the opportunity'.

Doulton Stoneware

From a paper read by John Sparkes to the Society of Arts, printed in the *Journal of the Society of Arts,* XXII (1874), pp. 557 - 566.

It is right at the outset of this paper to say, that the ware with which the recent revival of art interest in Lambeth is concerned is stoneware, a peculiar product of the potter's art, a kind of ware sufficiently difficult to define. I take it, however, that the definition from the official hand-book to the Exhibition of 1851 is accurate in general terms. It stands thus — "Stoneware is a dense and highly vitrified material, impervious to the action of acids, and of peculiar strength; it differs from all other kinds of glazed earthenware in this important respect, that the glazing is the actual material itself fused together". In Staffordshire, stoneware is always considered to mean a vitreous impermeable body. A porous body is never admitted to be stoneware. . . .

Stoneware is fired and glazed in one operation. During the first firing, which converts the brittle, useless clay into impervious ware, and when an intense white heat is reached, salt is thrown into the kiln, either from above, through holes in the crown of the kiln, or into the fire-holes, or both. The intense heat decomposes the salt, which is changed into a gaseous fume or steam. One constituent of the salt, the chlorine, escapes out of the kiln as vapour. Another portion however, the soda, as it flies through the kiln, meets with the white hot ware, in which is always a portion of silex or flint, and forms with it a silicate of soda, or soda glass. This subtle aëry glazing is thin, transparent, intensely hard, and almost indestructible, and does not coat the finest line or scratch so thickly as to obliterate it. It is on this account, from an artistic point of view, the perfection of glaze.

But the disadvantages are numerous. Few colours can stand the trial they are subjected to in the intense heat. The ware is brought, by the same agency, into a pasty softened condition in the kiln; this almost necessitates the sometimes clumsy thickness of the vessels made in stoneware, for very thin ones often lose shape seriously.

The more or less accidental impact of the fire, which has its currents of more or less intense heat streaming through it from the fire-hole to the crown of the kiln, produces various unforeseen effects on the colour of the ware, and on the colour of the pigment used in its decoration. The accidental path taken by the salt in its downward course from the crown of the kiln to the ware also produces great and unanticipated results in the colour of the ware, and leads to a bleaching or washing out of even strong colours, such as cobalt, which not unfrequently changes to grey or brown under the excitement of this downpour of chemical matter. It may be noted that a certain security against imperfect burning is attained by salt glazing, inasmuch as the salt will not volatilise at a lower temperature than suffices to make the ware white hot.

Such is the method of glazing stoneware with salt, which has been practised for hundreds of years. . . . . . .

The history of the more recent developments of stoneware decoration is this. In 1854, the Lambeth School of Art was established by Canon Gregory, with the intention of giving his parishioners a means of gratifying their taste for drawing in its most elementary form. It was thought that the potters of Lambeth would take advantage of their opportunities in this matter. This part of his plan, however, cannot be said to have come to any large practical result, as only one potter entered the school.

In 1856 I took charge of the school, and through the introduction of my potter student obtained access to some of the Lambeth kilns. I made a series of experiments with the view

XIV   Vase, earthenware. Ruskin Pottery (W.H. Taylor). Height 12ins. Dated 1922.

XV   Vase, earthenware. Ashby Potters' Guild. Height 4¾ins. Circa 1910.

of ascertaining whether colouring matter could not be made to adhere into incised lines, and whether the principle of stopping out, with a greasy pigment, that should dissolve and disappear in the kiln, could be applied. These and other experiments all answered to a certain point, and only wanted the practical energy of a manufacturer interested in the artistic perfection of his ware to have been brought to a successful issue.

A few years later I obtained an introduction to the firm of Messrs. Doulton, and was able to assist them in the execution of certain heads which were modelled in the Art School by Percival Ball, who subsequently obtained the highest distinction in the Royal Academy, and is now a rising sculptor in Florence.

After this, the Paris Exhibition of 1867 made its demand on the skill and enterprise of the English manufacturer, and the firm made some jugs and ornamental forms of vases with extra care, but with no great attempt to produce any work of the highest class. It was at this period that Mr. Edward Cresy, a friend of Mr. Doulton, suggested several of the forms and gave designs for some of the jugs that were sent to Paris. His culture and high taste enabled him to suggest to Mr. Doulton the line that the decoration of his material should naturally take. I am glad to be able thus publicly to acknowledge the deep obligations I owe to his ready aid, his accurate knowledge, his practical grasp of all questions of art or industry. The character of the ware exhibited in Paris was perhaps due to the fact that the highest practical excellence in manufacture had been reached. Vessels indispensable to chemical manufactories of the country, and others valuable as useful additions to the comforts and necessities of household demands, were produced at this time with a perfection in manufacture never before attained.

But the art-field was as yet uncultivated. A few desultory experiments made by scratching the green clay, done by two or three students of the Art School, were always being made. These are all lost; but comparatively simple as the ware in the Paris Exhibition was, it attracted wide recognition, which stimulated Mr. Doulton's efforts to further production. This hearty recognition of the attempts to ornament a simple material was, no doubt, due to the fact that the utmost simplicity of means was prescribed, and for the most part a graceful form was covered with concentric lines of parallel "runners" . . . .

The experience thus gained, through the friendly criticisms of the foreign press, was soon to be utilised. The first International Exhibition at South Kensington, in 1871, was the spur to new trials. The necessity of producing patterns really artistic, but with the full recognition of the colour and peculiar character of the Lambeth ware, led to the adoption of the scratching in of patterns on the ordinary brown stoneware body and filling in the scratched lines with colour.

The exhibition of these simply-decorated wares attracted attention, and the critics, and amongst them I believe Mr. Drury Fortnum, called the production Sgraffito ware. It was found convenient to retain the name; it had the recommendation of describing the method used in its decoration. This early name has been supplanted by another. The whole class, whether scratched in lines or ornamented by applied forms, is now called Doulton ware.

The various plans open to the artist in producing the effects you see here attained are briefly these:-

1. By scratching in the pattern while the pot is still wet, very soon after it is removed from the thrower's wheel. The line is scratched with a point which leaves a burr raised up on each side. This is useful, and serves to limit the flow of any colour that is applied, either within the pattern or to the ground that surrounds it.

2. At a later period, when the vessel has left the wheel twenty-four hours, the clay is too hard for this treatment. In this condition a burr is not turned up, but breaks off and leaves a broken blurred edge. When in this state the ware is scratched with an implement which scoops out a line, and delivers the clay that is removed cleanly away

from the cut. It makes a clear incised depression, with no burr; it too has its own beauty and subserves a use. Colour applied to the pattern, or to the ground, flows into it, fills it up, and is darkened by its deeper thickness at the place where a line crosses it.

3. Carving away a moulding or collar that is left on the ware by the thrower or turner is a fruitful source of excellent light-and-shade effects. This system is not only applicable to mouldings but also to flatter members, as for instance, where a row of leaves is first turned in a mass and carved in detail.

4. Another method is by whitening the body. But the material used for this purpose is of too short a texture to allow of ornamentation by the first method, viz., by scratching the wet clay with a point when half-dry; however, it is tough enough to be decorated with patterns taken out with the excised line. In this body we observe a difference from the ordinary brown ware body. It has a less affinity for the soda in the process of glazing with salt. It does not shine with the full glaze, as the brown ware does; and it has what is called a "smear" by potters. On the other hand, it takes the blue colour much more kindly, from the circumstance that the yellow or burnt sienna-coloured body of the ordinary ware is absent, and also that a certain natural relationship exists between the blue grey of the body and the deeper cobalt blue with which it is decorated. There is a harmony of likeness between them. This, too, is doubtless the cause of the pure deep blue on the old Rhenish ware.

5. Another system becomes imperative when a vessel of ordinary dark brown clay is dipped into a slip, or coating, of a white colour. It is obvious that a cut made on such a vessel would expose the brown colour of the body made visible by the removal of the white covering. This method offers many varieties of treatment, with or without the addition of colour to the cut surface.

6. Now, in addition to those various methods, there is still another, which was extensively used by the old Rhenish potters; it is by the application of dots, discs, flowers, borders, etc., by a process of sealing on a form of clay usually of a different colour from the ground, from a mould, much in the same way as the impression of a seal is made in wax, with this difference, that the clay seal is made to adhere to the surface on which it is pressed; the clay (or wax) being spread on the seal, not on the ware (or paper).

7. Similar in principle is the method of cutting in patterns from a mould; such lines of sharp environment serve to set bounds to the little rivulets of flowing colours, when fused and fluid by the intense heat of the kiln; they seem to limit the flow, which, if not thus checked, would run down the surface of the vessel.

8. Again, it is quite possible to stamp or seal on a disc or series of dots with such a material that it will burn away with the fierce heat, and leave a small circular inlay of beautiful crystallised brown-grey substance, flush with the surface of the ware. This method opens up a new field of decoration not yet developed.

These eight heads of methods seem to classify the schemes of decoration applied to the Doulton ware up to the present time, but scarcely a kiln is burnt off that does not yield a suggestion of a new line of trial for new systems, and these are stored to be taken up in the future as the demand for newer methods is made.

In the course of the growth of this new branch of manufacture, there have been one or two clear principles laid down for the guidance of all engaged in it. One is, that there shall be no copy of old work. We have taken old work, it is true, as our guides as to processes, as to the methods of scratching in of patterns, as to the sticking on of dots or bosses, and as to the plan of colour, but there our dependance on the old work has ceased. The endeavour has been constant to work on the principles observed in the works of the old potters, to use their experience in their treatment of soft clay, to start with all the advantage their practice gave us, but to imitate nothing.

XVI   Jar and cover, earthenware. Mortlake Pottery (George J. Cox). Height 4½ins. Dated 1912.

The second principle was to make no duplicates. It was felt that the art value of each piece would be found in the thought and skill bestowed on it. Neither thought nor skill, nor the finest perception of beauty, can make their mark on a piece of pottery that is mechanically reproduced. Thus each piece is unique, and its artistic value is not, nor ever can be lessened by the repetition of its decoration on the same or other forms. The sole exceptions to this rule are found when a pair of vases is required, or when a copy of a fine piece is required to make good the loss of the original.

It is the deliberate aim of all, those who plan the work and those who execute it, to bring about the greatest amount of variety and originality; but other causes besides deliberate intention come into play to aid us in giving the originality to the ware we so much desire to see. These are accidental, from numerous causes difficult to classify; more or less exposure to the fire, more or less shelter from a draught in the kiln, more or less salt in the glazing process; all these causes, and others, may, and do sometimes set at nought the most elaborate plan of colour, and ruin the best intentions. But there is a set off in this, for it not unfrequently happens that some of the very best effects of colour we have obtained have come from the partial burning away of the pigment. It is especially beautiful when the blue burns at the edges, and comes from the kiln with its exposed edges, fading into green or brown. These accidental effects are often exquisite . . . .

The artist who has given to the new ware one of its strongest characters is Miss Hannah B. Barlow. She was introduced to me some six years ago, by Miss Rogers, a lady who has written a most charming little work on "Domestic Life in Palestine", and the daughter of Mr. Rogers, the well-known wood-carver. An artist herself, she had an artist's quickness to perceive that her young friend, Miss Barlow, was destined to do good work in art. Miss Barlow's quick sketches of . . . . . creatures . . . . . show an intense feeling for the spirit of the beasts and birds represented. These etched out figures are, so to speak, instantaneous photographs of the animals. She possesses a certain Japanese faculty of representing the largest amount of fact in the fewest lines, all correct, and all embodying in a high degree the essential character of her subject. Yet there is little tendency to run into a picturesque treatment, but the fitness of her work for the manufacture, the recognition of the limitations under which the designs are made, are eminently kept in view in all her work . . . . .

Miss Florence E. Barlow, sister to the lady I have just mentioned, is another lady who gives great promise of a gift for animal drawing. Her work is at present somewhat undeveloped. . . .

Another lady artist is Miss Emily J. Edwards. Her work is ornament, made up of an ingenious mixture of classical or conventional forms with natural growths. There is usually great flatness of treatment in her work, with which elaborately diapered backgrounds in no wise interfere. The colour clings to the small stamped patterns on these backgrounds, and flows into the deeper depressions, to the manifest enrichment of the piece. She often gives indication of close study of antique methods of decoration . . . .

Another artist, whose skill has done very much for the ware I am describing, is Mr. Arthur B. Barlow. He has taken an entirely different line from that followed by his sister. His ornament is original — a flowing, tumbling wealth of vegetable form wreaths around the jug, now and then fixed by a boss, or pinned down by a point of modelled form. His education in the Art School as a modeller has been of vast assistance to him, and has given him many methods of dealing with the plastic form that comes under his hands. The occasional use of a gouge, or carver's chisel, or other carving tool, gives frequent evidence of what resources are his. He, too, has carried the system of bossing, or stamping with points, dots, and discs to its fullest development. His good taste and perfect mechanical ingenuity have carried his art into fields of decoration of unexpected beauty. . . .

Another artist who has made his mark on the ware by the originality of his forms, is Frank A. Butler. He is quite deaf and almost dumb. He is one of many thus heavily afflicted who have passed through the school. He began his artistic life as a designer of stained glass, but his invention was not needed, nor, I dare say, discovered in the practice of an art which is almost traditional. I introduced him to the new work, and in a few months he brought out many new thoughts from the silent seclusion of his mind. A bold originality of treatment and the gift of invention, are characteristic of his work. He has struck out many new paths. A certain massing together of floral forms, and ingenious treatment of discs, dots and interlacing lines indicate his hand ......

The artist who has done greatest service to the arts of all kinds in Lambeth is George Tinworth. He was originally brought up as a wheelwright under his father's mastership. He had early tendencies to be a sculptor. These were shown by his untutored carvings of Garibaldi and other heroes of the time. The carving of these things formed the occupation of his midnight leisure. His father, deeming these works of art dangerous, as likely to prove a bar to the proper attention his son ought to give to his wheelwright's business, broke them to pieces whenever he found them. An arduous childhood has educated in him a deep patience which has borne wonderful fruit. After his father's death, he tried to carry on the business single-handed, but he was unsuited to the work, mentally and physically. He had entered the Art School some time before this, and I was happy in being able to introduce him to Mr. Doulton as a modeller suited to his needs. His first works were some large medallions modelled from some Syracusan and Terina coins. These were done with astonishing spirit. When the demand for artistic stoneware came, his general grasp of the intention enabled him to do works that were more than equal to the occasion, and since that time he has done some of the best pieces the factory has produced. He prefers the clay soft from the thrower's wheel, so soft as to be too tender to handle. His delight is a spiral band or ornamental ribbon, sometimes deeply interdigitated, or elaborately frilled. The ornament usually covers as much surface as the ground, and creeps or flies over the surface in wild luxuriance; bosses, belts or bands of plain or carved moulding keep this wild growth to its work, put it in its place and subject it to its use. No two pots are alike, and although he has done quite a thousand, all different, he will still produce them in endless variety out of the same materials. Of course no one could produce such ever new combinations unless he had invention ......

I have said that the utmost care and the greatest artistic skill would be simply valueless if the actual details of manufacture were not equally cared for. This, however, has been done in a remarkable manner by those by whom Mr. Doulton has surrounded himself, for from the foreman, Mr. Bryant, who has selected and mixed the clays for the bodies, downwards, all have worked with most zealous spirit. All that has been accomplished in colour is due to Mr. Rix, who, by incessant experiments and cautious intelligence has produced blues and browns which equal the ancient ware, and are in some senses superior to them. He has also introduced some new tints, notably a pink and green, which have the rare merit of withstanding the intense heat of stoneware kilns and the decomposing vapours of the salt. He too, has organised the class of young girls who do the subordinate part of the work, such as the sealing on of dots and bosses, and has thus rendered it possible to produce these highly finished hand-works at reasonable prices. . . . .

The forms on which all this elaboration and decoration is placed are first "thrown" on the potter's wheel. The art of throwing is in danger of becoming extinct in Staffordshire, and was in use in Lambeth principally for the purpose of producing only the simplest wares, such as ink bottles, blacking bottles, jars, &c. The demand for beauty and accuracy of form found its supply in the works of Thomas Ellis, who has thrown all the forms. . . . His most skilful handicraft has done not a little to help on the fame of the new ware.

Many of [the] forms . . . . . are thrown roughly on the wheel, and then when green hard are shaved, that is, are turned in a lathe; this gives them a fine, true, highly polished surface. In this part of the process accuracy of hand and eye are both demanded. The earlier forms were shaved by Robert Atkins, who unfortunately died. His successor, George Martin, who has put the final surface on many . . . . examples . . ., has done his work in the spirit of an artist.

But as I have before remarked, the skill of the thrower, the handiness of the turner, the gifts of the artist, the knowledge and science of the colourist, are all in vain if the intelligence which keeps guard over the kilns, where all these works of beauty are tried in the fire, is unequal to the tasks of urging the heat to the proper pitch of intensity, of staying his hand when this has been attained, of knowing by instinct, as it appears to me, when the critical instant has arrived when the ware will take the salt. The gift of thus piercing the secrets of the fiery furnace, whence emerge either things of beauty that live for ever, or amorphous masses of "wasters", belongs eminently to William Speer. He spares himself no sacrifice of comfort or health to give up from the kilns the objects of loveliness that have been entrusted to his care to pass through the most critical period of their existence in the white heat of the furnace.

The Development of Lambeth Stoneware and Faience

From a paper read by John Sparkes to the Society of Arts, printed in the *Journal of the Society of Arts*, XXVIII (1880), pp. 344 – 355.

In May, 1874, I had the honour to read a paper in this place on the new methods that had recently been introduced into the Lambeth Pottery. I now propose to carry on the history of what has proved no inconsiderable development of the beginning recorded in that paper . . . .

The state of the manufacture was, perhaps, more remarkable for the freedom from disaster than for the uniform success that now may be said to characterise the productions of the kilns. Various improvements in detail, especially in the setting of the ware in the kilns, a better experience in the firing, gained by the practice of burning for Doulton ware, which formerly took its chance among the miscellaneous contents of the kilns, tend to this higher percentage of success; but, in the details of the decoration, and, to some extent, of the manufacture, great advance has been made. . . . .

By far the most important introduction has been a method of decoration, to describe which a French term has been used. It is called "pâte sur pâte". . . .

This very beautiful material was produced to show at the Paris Exhibition of 1878, and has been worked since with great success. To paint with the earthy pigment requires great decision of hand and accuracy; and, as each touch with the brush delivers the exact amount needed for the leaflet or digitation of the foliage used, it requires much practice and unerring certainty in planting the material on the ware firmly and in the right place.

The peculiarity of the method has produced a certain conventionality in the decoration, and a crisp-leaved sort of parsley-fern pattern seems to be the one mostly adopted. . . . . . .

There are eighteen colours and tints which can now be used in these ways — giving a possibility of infinite variety and endless combinations of colour and form. . . . .

Another very beautiful source of decoration is due to the manipulation of the clay, while still plastic, in the recently thrown form. . . . .

This goes . . . . to the extent of shaping the object afresh; for example, out of a circular bowl, as thrown on the wheel, we have a square one, or a polygonal one, or an elliptical one, or a shape combining all these forms. On these shapes, again, we have depressed grooves in rings, or in upright series, or in spiral windings, and these, crossed by others, giving a most pleasant variety of surface and of light and shade; and, again, no two can possibly be alike and all are the immediate product of the artist's mind. No mechanical process comes between him and his plans; he presses as far and as deeply as he wishes. and then treats these grooves to an ornament that will be appropriate to them.

The two artists who have done most to work out this beautiful decoration are two that I have mentioned . . . . George Tinworth and Frank Butler. . . . . .

A section that has always appeared to me to be most valuable, and one to be encouraged by all means in our power, is this, where the designer models on the piece that the thrower makes. . . . .

There are . . . . examples of this plan of modelling on the ware itself which will prove the position I take, viz., that it is a stimulus to individuality, and comes as a change from the etching or cutting-in of a pattern, in which some ladies — notably, Miss Barlow — excel; she occasionally feels that she can best express her intentions by a modelled figure of an animal in low relief, and is, of course, quite free to do this, or adopt any other method she chooses. . . . .

As to the artists who have worked so zealously to forward this great artistic manufacture, I can name certain of them who excel their neighbours, by reason of their greater opportunities and longer practice. . . . .

George Tinworth, whose name is widely known as a modeller of religious art that is quite unique of its kind, has lately executed a relief for the reredos for York Minster, and some excellent reliefs for the Guards' Chapel in St. James's park. . . . .

Frank A. Butler has developed into a master mind in his handicraft. He not only produces designs for himself, but keeps three or four assistants busy by designing forms and patterns for them to carry out. His best work, perhaps, is that where the ground is carved, leaving the pattern in relief and he is *facile princeps* in the treatment of the wet clay vessel, by squeezing it into shapes such as I have mentioned. . . . .

Miss Hannah Barlow also continues to give those clever and beautiful etchings of animals, which have such a concentrated spirit of observation in them as to seem inspirations from the very nature of the beast she is depicting. She has occasionally added rustic figures to the flocks and herds, with more or less success.

Her sister, Miss Florence Barlow, covers a more extended field, as she takes both ornaments and animals, and has recently executed some very charming paintings in coloured clays — of birds especially, which give a conventional light and shape and colour treatment to her desires, very helpful on the score of variety. . . . .

I now wish to add a few names . . . . to those previously given.

First among those who have thrown their whole energy into their work is Miss Eliza Simmance. Her work is not only designing with the stylus, but, especially she excels in painting the "pâte sur pâte" patterns. There are examples of her work . . . which are so eminently graceful and well-drawn as to emulate the same qualities in the work of the Italian ornamentists. She, too, has so many ideas to spare — more than she can work out by herself — that she keeps a staff of rising artists occupied in carrying out her instructions. . . . . . .

Another lady, Mrs. Eliza S. Banks, has taken up the painting on stoneware by the "pâte sur pâte" method, and has invented and executed some excellent designs on a larger and more picturesquely ornamental scale than anyone else. Her work is recognisable by a certain freedom of brush work, which, perhaps, occasionally verges on the natural side of the line that is conventionally held to divide nature from ornament.

Then, Miss Louisa E. Edwards may be taken as representing a style of decoration taken remotely from the Indian and Persian conventional flowers, but drawn with clear lines of perfect construction, and distributed with judicious thought, taste, and skill . . . . . Associated, to a certain extent, with her is Miss Louisa J. Davis, who has had considerable influence in a certain direction in enlarging the plan of treatment of the same Persian or Indian motives in their stoneware translation, and has treated certain natural plants — notably, reeds, sedges, and grasses — with a masculine vigour and power of drawing that remind one of old Gerard's woodcuts.

Also, Miss Edith D. Lupton has worked out some very characteristic half-natural forms, that in their distribution and grace leave nothing to be wished.

Miss Frances E. Lee has taken almost all sections under her care, and it is a little difficult to say in what she especially excels. She has taken up the method of pressing form into the wet clay, and has hit upon some fortunate combinations of this with surface ornament. Some of her simply incised surface decorations, also, are very good in their flatness.

Miss Mary Mitchell has lately begun to add outline incisions of rustic figures, treated with a pleasant semi-classical simplicity that promises well in the future. . . . .

In all the separate links of this art manufacture, the one great characteristic — the individuality of the artist — is carefully preserved, and there are, in consequence, just as many ideas as there are designers to embody them. No one is working out another person's design who has any power of his own. It is, I venture to say, in this way that the interest and the character of the ware is kept up. . . .

I now come to a second part of my subject, that of Lambeth *faïence* and *impasto* ware. *Faïence* is a convenient term for any sort of earthenware that is not white. It is so called either from trade-name association with Faenza, where majolica was largely manufactured in the 16th century, or from a French town on the Mediterranean coast with a similar name. It is a name borrowed from the French, and, like many other borrowed things, never returned to the proper owners. The name really has no clear meaning, but is a conventional term for painted pottery, on any ordinary natural clay as a body. Such pottery was produced in the Middle Ages exclusively, until the Italian potters of the 15th century borrowed from the Moorish potters of Spain the receipts for tin enamel. From this time, the tin enamel ware was used, almost to the exclusion of the *faïence* ware, for artistic and useful purposes. By this discovery, which poor Palissy broke his heart to find out (and which, by the way, he could have learned from any Italian potter, if he could but have met him, and induced him to talk on the subject), any common body of clay — a tile or brick, for instance — could be covered with an opaque shining skin, on which the artist could paint with any colour he desired to use. This was very beautiful but wore very badly, and the finest specimens are and were ornamental articles of luxury, carefully preserved until this day, and now may be seen in considerable abundance in every museum in Europe, and notably at the South Kensington Museum. Of this material is the so-called Rhodian ware, and several other kinds celebrated in their different localities. This ware held its own, together with various kinds of glazed earthenware, or so-called faïence bodies, until the discovery of china clay, which was made, not simultaneously, but within a few years of each other, by chemists in Germany, England, and France. The importation of porcelain from China and Japan had already partially spoiled the sale of the Italian and French productions, and the manufacture of porcelain itself in Europe put an end to the ware altogether.

The perfect surface of porcelain and its semi-vitreous fracture and imperviousness, and its white colour, gave it at once the place it so properly holds in universal esteem for household uses. The ordinary white earthenware of Staffordshire and other potteries is an imitation of porcelain, and is so good for common every-day use and so cheap, that it must be long before it meets with a rival in the markets of the world. But the perfection of the material did not lead to any very high class decoration; china painting in Europe almost entirely went wrong, inasmuch as artists were attracted by the perfect surface to paint miniatures on it, and in no china that I am acquainted with has an attempt been made to rival the large and decorative treatments that the material received in China, Japan and Persia.

The small and exquisitely-finished productions of the European porcelain factories were eminently unsuitable for the decoration of the walls of our rooms. Hence the demand for a better, larger, more comprehensive treatment of *plaques* and panels, which should be of harmonious colour, not too elaborated, simply, and more artistically, treated than could be expected from workshops or potteries where trade limitations of ideas prevailed. Again, there was a demand for colour, which the glaring white ground of earthenware bodies (much used for tiles) did not satisfy. Hence the reintroduction of our present faïence bodies and their popularity; the colour of the natural clay, not whitened, forms an agreeable base of operation for the painter; the range of colours is sufficiently extensive to do anything with, and, by the union of under-glaze colours with enamel, or over-glaze treatment, any colours whatever can be used.

This material has been taken into the service of the Lambeth pottery, and it has been with the desire to keep its range of decoration somewhat limited to the lines I have just sketched, that no great over-elaboration has been attempted. It allows of decoration, from the simplest expression of ornamental form to the finish of a miniature, and is equally fitted to form the base of a tile decoration, at two or three shillings a foot, as of the body of a vase, that will sell for several pounds. The examples . . . show the great range of effects that different treatments give. For instance, ... Lambeth imitations of Persian and Rhodian designs are perfect in their way, in good taste, well drawn, and a Lambeth translation of the originals not slavishly copied, but the differences of base, glaze, and pigment, have been frankly admitted, and the best made of the materials in the new line. The result is an intelligent work of art, charming in its harmony, and an ornament to any wall it can be applied to. The same may be said of . . . . landscapes, where the artist has accepted the limitations imposed on her by her materials, and seeks, not unsuccessfully, to produce effects bounded by these limitations. Again, I wish to point out that anything like over-elaboration has been carefully avoided; the effect of a *plaque* as a whole, on the wall, is what has been kept before the mind of the painter; that effect, as a piece of colour or tone, being achieved, the detail is done as well as it can be, consistent with this limitation. So with figures . . . . The effort to paint a head from nature, true to the model, would necessarily fail, from the uncertainty of the fire and the difficulties of the pigment. Therefore, we say, let the head or figure have as much character as possible, but let the colour be first decorative and large in treatment, and afterwards as well drawn and as probable as possible. On these lines, I conceive we have avoided slavish copies on the one hand, and mere incoherencies on the other, and have obtained *plaques* that may, at least, claim to be good decoration. So also with the landscape and figures combined. Thus it is with several selections of design founded on the Japanese and Chinese artists. A liberal interpretation of the meaning of the originals has been made in the transcript, so that the character of the Lambeth ware is not lost in any false effort to realise effects obtained in a material unlike itself.

The ware that is, on the whole, most capable of receiving artistic impressions is that which is called *impasto* ware. It is so named from the special treatment it receives at the hand of the artist who decorates it. The colour is applied to the raw clay; it is, further, so thickened by the vehicle by which it is incorporated, that it models the forms as well as paints it. The small amount of relief that is thus given the ornament — coloured, as it is — adds to the apparent reality of the thing depicted, and is, no doubt, an additional power in the hands of the artist; it is also a snare, inasmuch as the treatment of this principle involves a knowledge of modelling, to some extent at least. And, without some acquaintance with practice of light and shade, it is quite possible to produce a design devoid of effect; too evenly distributed all over the place. But with taste and judicious use of the raised parts, this new material may add very considerably to the pottery painter's means of producing good work.

The command over the texture as well as the tint of the background is also a point to be noted, as the application of paint, which has considerable opacity of substance, gives a quality that is never reached by half transparent films.

The whole system is, to a certain extent, analogous to painting with opaque colour in oil, while the average pottery underglaze painting is very like the water-colour painting, where the reflection from the ground passes through the coloured tints and films of pigment that cover it. *Impasto* painting, therefore, has all the advantages that opaque *tempera*, or oil painting, possesses; it reflects light from its surface. The opportunity this raised or *impasto* work gives for a second colouring, with underglaze colours, is to be remarked as rendering the work of art capable of taking a refinement of finish in detail on the surface prepared for it in relief. . . . .

In 1874, this large and important art section was only just taken up; therefore, no artists' names were at that time associated with the work. It is now a pleasant duty to mention the names of some who have done well by their taste, good painting, and designing, and who have impressed their individuality on the work.

Miss Florence Lewis has a remarkable power of design and skill in painting, that is seldom surpassed. Her designs are of foliage, flowers, and birds; and, whether she is working out a large design or a small tile, her energy and power are equally shown. . . . . Her sister, Miss Isabel Lewis, also gives great evidence of taste, although her original design suffers a little by the close comparison with her sister's.

Miss M.L. Crawley has made an important section her own. She early studied the Persian and Rhodian ornament, and now produces these beautiful examples of similar style to the great originals just mentioned, with clear drawing and excellent colour and distribution.

Miss Mary Capes has done everything; an inventive artist who experiments, and follows up the results thus obtained in a truly scientific spirit. Natural or convenient forms, geometrical or conventional ornament, seems to be equally familiar to this lady's experience.

Miss Capes has developed an excellent section, that of painting on stoneware already finished, with a dip, or single or mixed colours, and fired in the salt-kiln, with enamel colours. Certain examples rival some of the best qualities of Japanese art. The combination of textures and colours is often singularly happy.

Miss Katherine Sturgeon has taken the section of figure design, with considerable results. The heads she is able to arrange with studies from the model, have a very great sense of beauty, and good colour and effect. . . .

Miss Mary Armstrong has translated original figure designs, by Mr. Marks, and other designers, with much delicate sense of beauty and good taste.

Miss Fanny Stable has taken the treatment of large surfaces by the Japanese as her model, and by the study of these great teachers, has succeeded in producing paintings of excellent interpretation of nature.

Miss Mary Butterton, too, has done very much in original design, mainly treatments of natural forms, often circumscribed by geometrical limits, that are quite suitable to the form of the vase to be decorated. A firm decision of drawing is quite observable in her work.

Miss Alice Shelly has done some excellent treatments of natural flowers and foliage.

Miss Euphemia A. Thatcher has taken a similar style, in obedience to the constant demand for natural forms.

Miss Alberta Green, Miss Matilda Adams, Miss Margaret Challis, Miss Helen A. Arding, and Miss M.M. Arding, may be mentioned as having done much that is graceful and good in various styles.

Miss Esther Lewis has done several landscapes from nature, from sketches in Wales, Switzerland, and other picturesque countries; they are entirely satisfactory, as broad, breezy representations of nature in quiet grey and warm tones. From any point of view they are equally good decoration and good art.

Miss Linnie Watt has a most distinguished gift for conveying the impression of a picturesque scene with rustic figures, in excellent colour and with artistic breadth of effect, quite admirable in its truth. Some of her works . . . . will speak for themselves to every artist who sees them.

The impasto painting was primarily developed by a very talented artist, Miss F.M. Collins, (afterwards Mrs. Vale) . . . . She, too, we regret to say, has passed away from this world's activities, but not before she had made her gifts appreciated, and her great intelligence valued at Lambeth, in the care she took in the working out of a new and untried section of pottery.

Her successor is Miss Linnell . . . . Her treatments are in the largest style, and seldom run into trivial details.

No mention of names would be complete if I were to omit a short meed of praise to Mr. Arthur Pearce, who is a most prolific designer, and an excellent draughtsman at the same time. He has worked steadily at the School of Art, until now he is mainly relied on to make all the drawings wanted at the potteries for stoves, fireplaces, and similar sections. . . . . .

Some Original Ceramists

An article on the Martin Brothers and Charles Brannam which appeared in *The Magazine of Art,* V(1882), p.443.

In that great and wide revival of art of all kinds which has spread during the last thirty years and more over the whole of the civilised world, there is no branch to which more skill and labour have been devoted than pottery. Not only have all wares of all times been reproduced with remarkable success, and old processes re-discovered, till it may be stated generally that the history of pottery from the earliest times to the present has been retraced, but the art has been distinctly advanced in many directions. New methods have been invented, new colours found, new systems of decoration started. In this revival no country has taken a more prominent or successful part than England. Such firms as Messrs. Minton, Messrs. Doulton, and the Royal Potteries at Worcester produce ware not only perfect in *technique* but of rare and original artistic merit, such as cannot be excelled by any nation in Europe. The large capital which they so wisely employ enables them to command the services of accomplished artists, whose names and whose merit (to their honour be it spoken) they do not endeavour to conceal. But besides these large factories there have sprung up here and there small and independent ones, founded by men of special talent in decoration, whose art-work deserves to be more widely known than it is. To certain of these original ceramists it is the purpose of this article to introduce such of our readers as have not already made their acquaintance. They are Mr. Robert Wallace Martin and his brothers, of Southall, and Mr. Brannam, of Barnstaple.

If Martin-ware and Barum-ware have not the transparency of porcelain nor the elaborately and costly ornamentation of Sèvres, both are pure and honest art-work. The genuine potters who produce these wares do not attempt to rival nature by modelling flowers in relief, petal by petal; nor do they use the body of their jugs and vases as a canvas on which to paint Turneresque landscapes. Even when decorated, their vases and jugs remain vases and jugs - their proper form beautified but not concealed, their use evident and unambiguous. In other words, they understand the principles and proper limits of decoration, which should always have regard to the shape and material and destined employment of the thing decorated. The brothers Martin make stoneware only, and glaze it with salt. Mr. Brannam makes ordinary porous earthenware covered with different coloured slips, and glazes it with lead. The Martins employ all kinds of decoration, from modelling in relief to flat painting; Mr. Brannam only one kind - viz. imposing a pattern in one slip on the ground of another, sometimes modelling it in extremely shallow relief, so that the flatness of the surface, and consequently the shape of the article as thrown on the wheel, are not perceptibly disturbed. In character "Martin" decoration is sculpturesque, architectural, and naturalistic in turns, and is far more varied than Mr. Brannam's; but Mr. Brannam has a gift for original patterns and the conventionalisation of natural objects specially suited for the decoration of pottery, and very rare in modern European art.

So very different and numerous are the descriptions and styles of Martin-ware that it is difficult to classify; but a certain rough division has been made in the choice of objects for our illustrations, and this will serve to give a fair notion of the leading artistic ideas which stimulate its production. Robert Wallace Martin, the founder and director of the works - in which he receives valuable help, both artistic and technical, from three of his brothers - began life as a sculptor's assistant, and did not take to pottery till he had not only achieved thorough skill in modelling, carving, and such matters, but also an independent reputation as a promising young sculptor. This training, which included the knowledge of architectural ornament, has determined the character of a good deal of the work now produced at the Southall Pottery - such as cornices, mantelpieces, and figures. Of the latter he has not yet produced many, but the few he has finished are almost unique in their way as statuettes in stoneware. Few potters have ever used this material for the purpose; but that it is not improper the clever, well designed bas-relief which heads this article sufficiently proves. In the first place stoneware does not require glazing at all, and if the clay be well prepared it will endure burning without any disturbance of its shape; and in the second, if glazed, the salt glaze is so thin and transparent (more like a polish than a superadded surface) that the finest and sharpest cutting is scarcely changed by it. In this little bas-relief there are three figures. At one end is the boy who turns the potter's wheel; at the other the "thrower," who is shaping a vase as it grows up under his fingers. In the middle is the "bench boy" in the act of making the "balls" of clay ready for the "thrower;" the lump beside him he has just "wedged" - the last operation on the prepared clay. It has been crushed and mixed and sifted, "slipped" and "pugged." The object of "wedging" - beating one piece upon another, and cutting through again and again with a wire - is to drive out any remaining air. The dull and lifeless colour of stoneware "biscuit," and the uncertainty which always attends firing at the enormous heat necessary to bake it properly, are, however, great disadvantages for figures which require so much artistic labour; and it is probable that Mr. R.W. Martin will prefer as a rule to use the old and beautiful substance of terra-cotta when he wishes to turn his purely sculpturesque designs into pottery. In this class may be mentioned with praise a large figure of a monkey, a group of deer, a ram's head, and a few small statuettes.

The next of our illustrations shows a group of grotesques, the result of his sculptor's skill applied to realise his dream as a humourist. In these curious imaginings Martin-ware has a true specialty. It is doubtful whether in Europe a quaint fancy has ever been so successfully indulged in work of a sculpturesque character since the days of gargoyles. In the middle of our group stands a wondrous bird, half owl, half spoonbill, a feathered sage of profound experience, but, like Major Bagstock, "sly, sir, devilish sly." He holds his head on one side for the better criticism of inferior creatures, and closes one eye after the most approved habit of connoisseurs — a Sam Slick and a Solomon rolled into one. He is designed appropriately to contain the weed of wisdom. On either side of him are two gaping boobies, one marine - a cross between a tadpole and a dolphin - the other amphibious and antediluvian. Both are of very complicated ancestry, but most decided character. To these silly ill-tempered creatures, with their vast but empty heads, is fitly assigned the duty of warming spoons. Between them meditates a pre-adamite armadillo, crimped like a cod to hold toast; and a strangely human jug completes a group of creatures like many things, and yet like nothing on this earth, but nevertheless admirably good company for one another. There is something so whimsically human in these fancies, they are so impossible and absurd yet so funny and attractive, that they remind us of nothing so much as the good old nursery rhymes. They are nonsense indeed, but good nonsense, which is even more difficult to carve than to write. It takes a wise man to be a fool of this calibre, and he would deserve to be

prized if only for his rarity. We have a hundred young sculptors who will model you a Venus or an Adonis as soon as look at you; but who save Mr. Martin who could give you a Boojum or a Snark in the round?

Our third and fourth groups are of beautiful shapes. These are produced by the two throwers Walter and Edwin Martin. If the former throws with greater accuracy and skill, the latter is quite his equal in invention, and is the creator of most of the smaller articles - little bottles and vases, cruets, and the like. With great industry and never-failing invention the brothers will go on producing vase after vase, no two alike, for hours together. Every one in the small establishment takes his share in the decorating. Some pieces are decorated with conventional ornaments, some with natural objects such as flowers and birds; some have raised modellings; some, like the large bottle in our illustration, are perforated, others are made more beautiful by outlines incised and filled in with colour. In short, there is scarcely any variety of decoration which is not employed; and the ornament is marked by the utmost liberty of invention consistent with due subordination to shape.

Crushed pottery is another of the Martin specialities: *e.g.,* the very comic jug in our second group. The sinking of a vase after it is thrown, or the "spoiling" of its shape during decoration, instead of condemning the vessel to destruction, often sets the ingenuity of the brothers at work. I have a bottle whose crushed sides are worked with a few dints and scratches into humorous suggestions of feline heads. On one side the animal is more like a tiger — a resemblance which is helped by black marks in the rich brown glaze; on the other side is a very tame cat. A bulge in another jug suggested suffering, and a few deft touches of the practised modeller were sufficient to indicate humanity without destroying its jug-like character; it is not a man's head with a spout, but a jug with a toothache. Another I have seen which was thrown too thin, and could not be lifted without "giving"; the fancy of the youngest brother Edwin turned this mischance into a victory, and repeating the crumplings at intervals, and decorating the vase with complete sympathy to its altered shape, produced a work of art at once strange and beautiful.

In these days, when the owner of capital so often gets not only the profit but the credit which is due to the artist, it is pleasant to be able to record a case in which men of independent talent and energy, aided only by such occasional good offices as most of us receive from our fellow-men, have made a career for themselves, and after struggles of no ignoble character have succeeded in establishing an art-factory of such high and distinct

character as the Southall Pottery. The following outline of the history of the Martin brothers may be trusted, as it is founded on information supplied by themselves.

Their father was a descendant of Thomas Martin, the antiquarian and historian of Thetford, and was born in Suffolk. He became the manager of a large woollen drapery establishment in Dublin when a young man; but a practical joke caused him such serious injury that he was obliged for the rest of his life to be content with inferior employment. The "joke" in question was the firing of a pistol close to his ear, which permanently injured his hearing. By the influence of his mother's sister, Mrs. Barry, he got work in the warehouse of Messrs. Barry and Hayward, wholesale stationers. He married the daughter of a Scotch baker, and had six sons and three daughters. Four of the sons — Robert Wallace, the eldest, born in 1843; Charles Douglas, the third; Walter Fraser, the fifth; and Edwin Bruce, the sixth — now form the firm of Martin Brothers. The regular education of Robert (or Wallace, as he is called by his brothers) was somewhat short and fitful, but allowed some opportunities for the discovery of his taste for Art. He went to the Birkbeck Schools in the City Road and Waterloo Road, at both of which were drawing classes. At eleven years old he astonished his parents by carving a child's head out of a small piece of chalk, and after trying work at a tailor's, a hatter's, a candle factory, and at Barry and Hayward's, he met with an accident, and on recovery determined to try for some artistic employment. His father, who on all occasions appears to have assisted his inclinations to the best of his ability, borrowed a statuette of a neighbouring mason, of which Wallace made a drawing. This was shown by the mason to the foreman of the late Mr. J.B. Phillips, an architectural sculptor with a studio in the Vauxhall Bridge Road. Here the boy was allowed to try his hand at stone-carving for some months, when, his family moving to the Mile End Road, Mr. Phillips offered to take him as a pupil for £50 and no salary for the first year. Though his mother offered the £50, he would not allow such a sacrifice of her little capital. Here his connection with his father's employers proved useful, for Mr. James Barry showed some of his drawings and carvings to his brother Sir Charles, the architect of the Houses of Parliament, who placed him without premium or conditions under his Gothic carver. Roughing out crokets and finials not satisfying his artistic ambition, he carved naturalistic leaves and flowers in alabaster in his leisure hours, and made a gallant attempt at modelling a figure of Samson, for which his willing father stood as a model in his bedroom. This finished, he next attempted to cast it in plaster: an effort which resulted in complete failure. He was more successful with his first commission, which was a life-sized medallion of a defunct neighbour, from a cutting in black paper. This earned him praise and the mighty sum of seven and sixpence. After modelling his father's bust and competing unsuccessfully for prizes offered by the Council of the Architectural Museum and the Society of Arts, he joined in 1860 the drawing classes in St. Mary's School, Lambeth. Next year, being then but eighteen years old, he determined to seek work personally of some famous sculptor. Rebuffed by Mr. Weeke's footman, he passed Mr. Munro's door without daring to knock. He summoned up his courage and tried Mr. Adams's knocker. Mr. Adams was out, so he went back to Mr. Munro, who received him kindly, set him to work "backing out" a marble bust, and employed him for seven years. During those years he did a good deal of original and successful work as a sculptor. In 1862 he modelled a bas-relief of a boy's head and shoulders (the portrait of his brother James) which was accepted at the Royal Academy next year. In 1864 he was admitted to the schools of the Royal Academy and gained the prize for an original design for a medal of merit for the South London Working Classes Industrial Exhibition, 1865, which was engraved in the *Illustrated London News*. He received one of his own medals as a first class prize for works in stone, plaster, and terra-cotta sent to this exhibition. In 1866 he carved a statue of Britannia for the County Fire Office, Canterbury, and gained prizes at the Exhibition of the Architectural Museum and the Society of Arts. In several subsequent years he exhibited at the Royal Academy and at the international and provincial exhibitions. His "Girl at the Spring," a charming alto-rilievo, was engraved in the *Art Journal* in 1875. Here for the present ends his chronicle as a sculptor. The bas-relief we have engraved shows that he has not altogether abandoned his first love; and it is to be hoped that as the pottery which he has set in motion exacts less pains and personal attention, he will come back to it with fresh ardour and a skill nowise prejudiced by the practice of decoration.

A boy who by strong will and steady work had gained a thorough education as a sculptor, without any money and with no loss of self-respect, was not likely to be easily discouraged in any venture. As we all know, sculpture in England is not a good art for a poor man; and it was probably because Martin wished to earn a better livelihood, while retaining the free use of his artistic gifts, that he resolved to turn potter. The idea was "in the air" of Lambeth, where — at the suggestion, I believe, of Mr. Sparkes, then head master of the Lambeth School of Art — Doulton had commenced his famous revival of decorated stoneware; and though Martin never worked for Doulton, and had no opportunity of studying the process of his manufacture, the design of his next enterprise was naturally generated by so near an example of beautiful work and profitable business. At all events he left Mr. Munro in 1868, and after trying in vain for some years at Lambeth to get at some of the secrets of pottery, he went on his travels. His first journey was to Devonshire, where he got employment as a modeller in an art-pottery for several months, and made a collection of clays; then he went to potteries in Staffordshire and elsewhere — "with his eyes open." On his return in 1872, he made an agreement with Mr. Bailey, the owner of the historic Fulham Pottery, which the Dwights made famous, to start art-work there. But the art-work did not pay, and the agreement soon ended; and he began to make stoneware on his own account, assisted by his brother Walter, a youth of sixteen, who had been employed by Doulton in the mechanical part of decoration — that is, in filling in with colour designs scratched on the unbaked clay. It was at Pomona House, King's Road, Fulham, that the brothers began that hearty co-operation which, after many years of difficulties bravely overcome, has resulted in the present family kiln at Southall, with a showroom and place of business in Brownlow Street, Holborn. At first they had no one who could throw; but Walter learnt throwing by practice first on a small and then on a large wheel, till he threw so well that they were suspected of employing a trained hand from another factory. Then Walter built a small kiln in the chimney, and succeeded in obtaining a salt glaze. Soon the other brothers Charles and Edwin joined them. Edwin had been employed at Doulton's on the same kind of work as Walter, and Charles, after a serious consumptive attack, had recovered his health in Devonshire, and had travelled for a dyer. Charles had had some artistic training, and Walter and Edwin had attended the drawing classes at the Lambeth School of Art. All the brothers seem to have fallen naturally into their places in the family co-operative association. Wallace, the eldest, assumed of course the direction, decorating, modelling, designing, and generally settling what was to be done and how to do it. To Walter was left entirely the management of the kiln, and at first the throwing; but he too decorated, and does so yet, with much skill and a fine sense of form and decorative propriety. He is also the "chemist" — always experimenting with colours — the engineer, and the mechanician. Edwin, the youngest, soon learnt the throwing, which he does swiftly and well, with never-failing invention; he paints the designs of others more quickly, and decorates with great skill and freedom. Charles is the man of business. He designs occasionally, and is fertile in suggestions of patterns and schemes of colour; but from the first he has been engaged in the more practical part of the concern: selling and taking orders, and generally developing the business with modesty and sagacity.

Their first burning was in an old crucible kiln a few miles from Fulham, which they had

to alter with their own hands so as to make it suitable for salt-glaze ware. They had also to make what are called "tiles" and "binders" (or generally "gear"), to form the cupboards or cells which are used instead of "saggers" in salt-glaze kilns. These being ready, besides "rolls" and "flat" (pieces of soft clay well sanded: "rolls" to put between the pieces of gear; "flat" to put under each piece of ware, to prevent all from sticking together in the burning), they tried the kiln first with terra-cotta only, and then with salt-glaze ware, which requires longer and fiercer burning. Both these experiments being fairly successful, they tried again; but then happened one of their misfortunes. The owner of the kiln had burnt crucibles in it between their two firings, and the consequence was that all their month's work was spoilt. This accident had well-nigh ruined the firm. The Fulham Pottery would no longer burn for them, and they could not burn for themselves; their stock in Brownlow Street was getting low, and their unburnt work was useless. They looked about for a place to build a kiln, and found the deserted soap-works at Southall, which is now the Southall Pottery. By the help of one friend they were able to buy the lease and plant, and to build their present kiln; by the aid of another, two years later, they were able to put up a building round it to protect it in the winter. Many other troubles they had, and the "works" are now small and rough enough to look at; but the Southall Pottery is an accomplished fact, turning out some 5,000 pieces in the course of the year, all manufactured by three brothers (with one clever assistant and a boy), from the crushing of the clay to the firing in the kiln. As an instance of what can be done by the energy of one dominating spirit and the strength of brotherly co-operation, the history of the brothers Martin should be encouraging to all men who desire to work out an independent career, in which their natural gifts may have free exercise.

Our illustrations of Barum-ware give some notion of the variety of shapes thrown in Mr. C.H. Brannam's pottery at Barnstaple, North Devon. This pottery came to him by inheritance, a sound and useful but not an artistic pottery. Such necessary articles as drains and roofing tiles made of the clay found on the spot were its principal manufactures. But Mr. Brannam attended the local school of art, and developed a strong artistic feeling, so that when the pottery descended to him it was not long before he began to make experiments in

decorative work. These were at first confined to small jugs and vases of ordinary shapes, made of red clay, covered with white "slip" in which patterns were neatly incised. About two years ago one of the partners of the well-known firm of Messrs. Howell and James, who is a Devonshire man, brought a few of Mr. Brannam's earlier attempts to London, and showed them to Mr. J. Buxton Morrish, another partner in the same firm. Mr. Morrish at once divined the talent and originality latent in the rough but artistic designs, and sent down his manager to Barnstaple to make definite proposals to Mr. Brannam — to assist him in developing his new ware, and to become his sole representative in London. Shortly after this Mr. Brannam visited London, where he conferred with Mr. Morrish, whose taste and experience were, I believe, of much value in suggesting variations as to shape and colour. Professor Church, who was then delivering his series of Cantor Lectures on artistic pottery at the Society of Arts, brought some specimens of Barum-ware before his audience; and the encouragement thus received was not lost, for Mr. Brannam has not only set his inventive faculty to work in producing many excellent and novel designs, but has greatly extended the range and improved the quality of his colour.

The character of the decoration and shapes of Barum-ware is shown in our cuts — of bottles and vases. Some of the vases are of considerable size and executed with skill. The designs consist of panels of various forms sympathising with the shapes of the vessels, and filled with conventionalised birds, fishes, and flowers, which show much fertility of invention and decorative ingenuity. The panels are separated by bold scrolls and zig-zags, and the corners and odd spaces filled up with globes, shells, and other plain and effective forms, which give the work an individuality of a somewhat archaic character: as though an early Egyptian or Trojan potter had transmitted his simple artistic feeling to his successor in Devon. As to his colour, in addition to the contrasts of white and red and brown and yellow with which he first started, Mr. Brannam now produces very soft and rich combinations of chocolate and blue, leaf-green, and pale yellow, and other secondaries and tertiaries. It is impossible to say of what other beautiful developments Martin-ware and Barum-ware are capable; but what the founders of these potteries have already accomplished is quite sufficient to entitle them to an honourable place in the list of England's original ceramists.

COSMO MONKHOUSE

Minton's Art Pottery Studio

G.W. and F.A. Rhead: *Staffordshire Pots and Potters* (London, 1906), chapter XXVI.

Towards the close of the 'sixties Mr. W.S. Coleman, who was a well-known illustrator and a capable watercolour painter, began to make experiments in the decoration of pottery, with a view to taking up pottery-decoration as a profession. Finding it inconvenient to pursue his experiments so far away as London from the scene of the practical working of pottery, he applied to Messrs. Copeland to give him the necessary facilities for furthering the scheme which he had in view, and went to Staffordshire forthwith. He does not appear to have been, in fact was not, satisfied with the facilities which Messrs. Copeland were able to offer him, for a few months later he made overtures to Mr. Colin Minton Cambell, who received him, so to speak, with open arms, and gave him the use of a commodious studio at the end of the china works overlooking the town of Stoke.

Mr. G.W. Rhead, who was then a lad of fifteen, and a young apprentice on the works, was sent to Coleman's studio for the purpose of giving him instruction in the practical working of pot colours. Coleman, however, made such rapid progress that he very soon began to teach his quondam instructor, and, during the year 1870 and part of 1871, produced a series of plaques, bowls, fireplace-slabs, etc., so charmingly fresh in character, so entirely different in treatment from anything previously seen in the Potteries, that they at once made a deep impression, even amongst the workers, who were not prone to the reception of new ideas, and who viewed with mistrust any innovation or departure from the beaten track.

Coleman's earliest work was done in under-glaze colours upon the bisque, and glazed by hand with the brush, not dipped, the painting being done with water as a medium and the glaze mixed with turps, so as not to disturb the painting. By this means he could distribute the glaze as he chose. The delicate parts of the painting, such as the flesh and faces of figures, would be glazed thinly, while cobalt blue, which is a strong colour, requiring and absorbing more glaze would be glazed more thickly. . . .

The examples which remain most clear in our memory (we shall never forget the impression on first entering the studio, and seeing these charming things ranged upon a shelf round the room) are a plate with a duck and ducklings, completely finished in under-glaze colours and glazed in a soft glaze, imparting a beautiful soft quality to the colours. This plate subsequently passed into the possession of a well-known connoisseur, Mr. Charles Magniac. A coarse earthenware plate with a cock and young chickens, vigorously drawn with what appeared to be a pen-line, and, of a somewhat later period, a charming head of a pretty child reclining on a couch, of which there are several versions, including a small trial tile, about 4 in. by 3 in. There were also a number of plaques of fanciful subjects of heads, some executed upon a body with a roughened, granulated surface, which he caused to be specially prepared. The work of this, his earlier, period, when he relied exclusively upon under-glaze colours, must undoubtedly be accounted the most satisfactory as pottery decoration, since the quality of under-glaze, which is the result of the complete fusion of the colours with the glaze, is superior to anything which enamel colours can give. Coleman, however, who was a born colourist, and had a preference for the brighter pigments, became impatient of the somewhat limited range which under-glaze colours afforded. He preferred the brilliant turquoise enamel (for which Minton's were famous) to the paler hues of the under-glaze. He even preferred the bright enamel blue to the more sober though infinitely more splendid tones of under-glaze cobalt. He therefore gradually abandoned the use of under-glaze colours, and his latest works were painted almost entirely in enamel colours with the exception of the strong brown outline, which was done under-glaze, and which was never abandoned, and occasionally one or two other colours, such as orange, which in under-glaze is very brilliant . . . . .

To the second period of Coleman's work on pottery belong two large fireplace slabs 3ft. 6in. by 12 in. painted with a peacock and a trogon, and drawn in his own inimitable style, both these subjects giving him ample opportunity for indulging in the brilliant tints which were so attractive to him.

About this time, during the year 1870, he painted what he always considered his *chef-d'œuvre* in pottery, a large plaque, about thirty inches in diameter, with tropical plants (American aloes, etc.), and a flying bird, with an orange background, a scheme of colour which he was very partial to, on account of the fine quality of the under-glaze orange. It was done in greater part under-glaze, but finished in enamel; unfortunately, as it turned out, the plaque, which was of unusual size, split in the enamel kiln. We well remember his exclamation of intense disappointment on his coming in the morning and finding the plaque in two pieces. It was an instance, so common in human experience, of the thing upon which we build our most cherished hopes being foredoomed, as it were, to failure.

We have now to direct the reader's attention to an important work in tiles done in London a year or two previous to the period which we have been considering. We refer to the decoration of the grill-room at South Kensington Museum, designed by Sir Edward, then Mr., Poynter, and executed by some of the lady students of the National Art Training School. It was the success of this work which led the authorities at South Kensington to consider whether some means could not be found for the establishment of an Art Pottery Studio in London which would provide employment for such lady students of the Training School as desired it. This was one of the numerous schemes which were mooted at the time for the employment of women of the middle and upper middle classes. Messrs. Minton, through whom the work in the grill-room and other important ceramic work in the Museum was done, were approached in the matter. A five-years' lease was granted by the Commissioners of the 1851 Exhibition, of a plot of land situated close by the Albert Hall, immediately between the Royal College of Music, which was then in process of construction, and the conservatory of the Royal Horticultural Gardens. A studio was erected upon this site, with enamel kiln for firing, and in the spring of 1871 was opened, under the art directorship of Coleman, having the twofold object of establishing a better standard of taste in pottery decoration, and, as previously stated, of offering an opportunity of remunerative employment to the students of the National Art Training School.

The studio was established under the happiest auspices. No project, surely, was ever launched with greater opportunities. It soon became one of the show-pieces of London, and was visited by a number of the most highly placed personages, amongst whom were the Crown Prince and Princess of Prussia (afterwards the Emperor and Empress Frederick), the King of the Belgians, the Marquis and Marchioness of Lorne, as well as many people distinguished in literature and the arts.

A number of students from South Kensington (the greater proportion ladies) were soon attracted to the place, and a variety of things were produced — plaques, vases, bowls, pilgrim-bottles, and tiles for fireplaces and other decorations, amongst the most successful of which were: the large plaque designed by Coleman referred to in the earlier portion of this chapter, of tropical plants and bird, with yellow ground, of which a number of replicas were made; a two-handled bowl, with three feet, about 12in. high by 15in. broad, the shape of which was designed by Coleman and decorated by him with fish and water-plants, this also being repeated a number of times; two "dragon" bottles designed, or rather adapted from the Japanese, by G.W. Rhead; a small long-necked bottle, also adapted by G.W. Rhead from a Satsuma vase in the South Kensington Museum; a pair of circular bottles with a flattened surface, about 18 in. high, decorated with plants and birds in turquoise and blue with black background, from designs by Coleman . . . . .

During this, the earlier period of the Studio, an important decorative work was carried out for Eaton Hall, Cheshire, the seat of the Duke of Westminster. This work includes a long horizontal fireplace slab with a frieze of figures in mediaeval costume, representing the signs of the Zodiac, designed by H.S. Marks, R.A. (of which a number of replicas were afterwards made); a series of panel slabs, illustrating Shakespeare's Seven Ages, painted in colours with gold background, also designed by H.S. Marks (of this series also a number of replicas were made); a large panel of tiles, for the bathroom, of tropical water-plants and birds, painted by G.W. Rhead from Coleman's design, and a number of smaller panels of plants on a buff ground.

It was about this time that the Criterion Theatre and Restaurant was being completed, and it was intended to decorate the restaurant with tiles. It was well understood that the proprietors, Messrs. Spiers & Pond, together with their architect, Mr. Verity, were desirous that Messrs. Minton should execute the work at the Criterion, they having had several of their restaurants decorated by Messrs. W.B. Simpson & Sons, and wishing for a change of style. Coleman therefore submitted a rough sketch of the general colour scheme which he proposed to carry out, together with an enlargement of one of the figures, a Cupid pursuing a butterfly, a favourite idea of his. It was sufficiently evident, however, that Coleman's heart was not in the work. He was engrossed with his plaques, for which he found a ready sale at prices varying from thirty to fifty pounds, and even more. He was rather of an indolent habit of mind, and seemed to avoid the mental effort necessary to the successful carrying out of an important decorative work. The commission was therefore entrusted to Messrs. Simpson, who carried out the work, thus depriving the Studio of an important opportunity which might very well have been taken advantage of.

About this period (the close of 1872) Mr. John Eyre, who is at present a prominent member of the Royal Society of British Artists, and an able painter in water-colours, and who at that time had recently completed his National Scholarship at South Kensington, had returned to Staffordshire, and was casting about for an opportunity of turning his abilities to account. Mr. Eyre made an application to Messrs. Minton, with the result that he was engaged to come to the Studio in London to assume the threefold duties of designer and painter and general overlooker or foreman, and to superintend the firing of the kiln, which had practically become a necessity to the Studio, on account of the various inconveniences incidental to the sending of the ware backwards and forwards to Stoke to be fired, which had been done up to this period . . . . .

Prominent amongst the ladies of the Studio was Miss Hannah Barlow, who had a considerable love for, and facility in drawing animals. Her interest in animals, indeed, was the source of much consternation among her feminine fellow-workers, from her habit of bringing mice, frogs, and other livestock to the Studio in her pockets. Miss Barlow . . . never found at the Studio an outlet for her artistic energies. After a comparatively short period she accepted an appointment at Doulton's, where she found in their grey stoneware a material which was exactly suited to her very individual talent.

During this time Coleman cotinued to produce his plaques, which increased in popular favour. The advent of Mr. Eyre as general overlooker was a convenience to him; it relieved him of a part of his responsibilities and enabled him to devote his time almost exclusively to his own work, in which he was obviously more interested. From this time he gradually lost touch with the Studio, and finally about the end of 1873, severed his connection with it entirely as Art Director, although he continued to send his work there for the purpose of being fired.

This event marked the close of the Studio's first and far more successful period. The work, however, was popular, and as a consequence the dealers continued their support. It was therefore necessary to appoint someone to fill the post which Coleman had vacated. This was done, in the person of Mr. Matthew Elden, a singular and wayward creature who originally hailed from the Potteries, had been the friend and fellow-student of the elder Kipling, and was one of Whistler's earliest and most enthusiastic supporters. Elden came to London at an earlier period in his career, and, during his connection with the Training School at South Kensington, took part in the execution of the modelled decorations then in progress for the façade of the new Wedgwood Institute at Burslem.... His work at Minton's Studio may be summed up in the one word *failure*. He was for ever experimenting: inventing devices for this and "dodges" for that. He introduced an odorator or "spray" for the purpose of laying flat tints of colour upon the ware, and tint upon tint, to produce "quality", and covered everything in the place with this system of tinting. If he happened upon occasion to achieve any measure of success, he couldn't rest apparently until he had spoiled it. He produced numbers of sketches, showing considerable power up to the point to which they were carried; but these were never carried beyond the sketch stage, and probably never intended to be completed. He was something of a hustler, even in those pre-hustling days, before the genus "hustler" had come into being, and even contemplated the partitioning of the place into stalls or pens, to prevent conversation between the workers, and thus obtain a greater proportion of work from each person. Elden's individuality was as strong in its own way as that of Coleman, but it is curious to note the difference in the tone and morale of the place which was brought about by the introduction of a different personality. The earlier period remains a pleasant memory to all who took part in it, and is in the strongest possible contrast to the ones which followed.

Another member of the Studio whose work possessed exceptional interest, was Mr. Edward Hammond, whose somewhat wayward character had some sort of affinity with that of Elden. Mr. Hammond produced among other things a set of tiles, of musicians in mediaeval costumes, somewhat after the manner of Marks, but finer in character. These designs were etched upon copper by Hammond in a strong outline, and were taken up at this stage by Elden, who supplied precisely that quality which Hammond was unable to impart, and, on the other hand, the outline possessed more character than Elden's work displayed. The union of the two men's work was therefore in this instance most happy, as each supplied what the other lacked. The tiles were produced in large quantities, the outlines printed from the copperplates, and the shading finished by hand. They were afterwards modelled at Stoke in low relief, and glazed with a blue or brown glaze. Of these also many were produced and sold....

The Elden regime lasted a matter of eighteen months or two years, during which period Mr. Eyre had seceded from the place, finding himself completely out of sympathy with Elden's methods. There was still another stage, which in many respects was even more unsatisfactory than the last. Messrs. Minton opened up negotiations with Colonel Stuart-Wortley, an exceedingly able amateur photographer, who took portraits of his friends (heads and figures; chiefly heads, however) in mediaeval and fancy costume. These were copied, on the imitative system, in large numbers upon large plaques, and very well copied too, from the imitative point of view. It will, however, be sufficiently obvious that this kind of thing had no sort of affinity with fine art. The photos were excellent, as photos, but, leaving unanswered the nice question as to whether photography has been helpful or harmful to art (for ourselves we are convinced that it has been entirely harmful, and at best is but a convenience), there is an unfathomable gulf between this and the great Italian traditions bequeathed to us by Gubbio, Urbino, and Castel Durante.

The move was a leap in the dark; it was one of those feverish actions which men take in a moment of stress and difficulty. Elden had left nothing but a legacy of failure and incompetence. Mr. Colin Cambell had arrived one morning to find a huge pile of bowls decorated with a coarse, vulgar design in far-off imitation of Coleman's beautiful fish-bowl, and "blown" upon by Elden's odorating process. These were sold *en bloc* to Messrs. Mortlock for thirty shillings each. Elden, finding that his own work did not particularly please, had fallen into the error of trying to imitate Coleman, instead of developing his own quite genuine individuality. The dealers were beginning, indeed had begun, to look askance upon the place, and the "photograph" was considered the panacea for all the ills that the Studio had become heir to. It is easy to see that the end could not be much longer delayed. The workers arrived one morning in the summer of 1875 to find the place reduced to a heap of ashes. The firing of the kiln was the cause, and the accident of the fire was seized upon as a decent excuse for closing the place . . . .

During what may be termed the "photographic" period, and by way of strengthening the Studio by the infusion of fresh blood, Dr. Christopher Dresser, who was a well-known designer and ornamentist of the neo-Gothic school of Talbert and Pugin, was invited to supply designs. Dr. Dresser produced a number of designs of a semi-humorous character, which, however, can scarcely be said fairly to represent his powers, which were very considerable. The only example which remains in our memory is a small circular bottle with a flat surface, upon which was represented a rencontre of two cats on a garden wall, with a moon behind . . . .

Minton's Studio was an interesting experiment which deserved a better fate. It produced during the earlier period a good deal of very excellent work. It directly created that interest or "craze" for pottery decoration which became almost universal throughout the country during the seventies, and, amongst a good deal of down-right bad work, a certain proportion of good work was done. Nearly everybody took up pot-painting for a time, and a considerable business was done both in London and elsewhere in the supply of materials and firing. It was indeed more than a craze; it became a positive fever. Almost any rubbish found a ready sale, and the character of the periodical exhibitions of amateurs' work at Messrs. Howell & James's, in Regent Street, led George Augustus Sala to exclaim in a spirit of righteous indignation, "Oh, for a good, honest kitchen poker!". The Studio attracted a number of very capable amateurs, amongst whom was Mr. A.B. Donaldson, who, however, being a water-colour painter of considerable originality and distinction, can scarcely be considered an amateur, but rather as a painter who took up pottery as a pleasant alternative to his work in water-colour. Mr. Donaldson produced a number of very interesting pieces. Mr. W. De Morgan, the well-known potter, was an occasional visitor to the Studio, but only for the purpose of taking advantage of the convenience of the enamel kiln. Mr. J.D. Rochfort was a man of leisure who adopted pottery purely as a recreation, and who also did good work.

Another important result which must not be forgotten is that Minton's Studio most probably, we may say certainly, provided the incentive to Messrs. Doulton to take up art work in pottery. It was the pioneer in London, although Messrs. W.B. Simpson had already been doing most excellent work, chiefly, however, in tiles.

The Fourth Annual Exhibition
of Paintings on China

A review which appeared in *The Magazine of Art,* II (1879), p. 269.

It is a gratifying task to us who are deeply interested in the success of a branch of art, which has only recently taken root in this country, to have to chronicle so decided an advance in the present exhibition over that of last year. We were compelled, in our notice on a previous occasion (vol. i., p. 176), to point out many faults and imperfections both in design and workmanship, and to show how we believed it was possible that improvements might be introduced; and we were agreeably surprised, on our recent visit to Messrs. Howell and James's galleries, to find that many of the weaknesses we had formerly to signalise have now disappeared, and that a marked numerical increase in the objects exhibited is accompanied by a most real and decided improvement in the quality and execution of the works. Ladies and amateurs have, indeed, every reason to strive for the numerous and valuable prizes freely offered by royalty, and for the opportunity of having their works so admirably displayed as they are in the well-arranged galleries in Regent Street. The list of patrons on the present occasion includes nearly every member of the Royal family, and Messrs. E.W. Cooke, R.A., and F. Goodall, R.A., have again acted as judges. The works of the principal amateur prize-winners have been separated from those of their companions, and are shown in a gallery on the first floor. The gold medal presented by the Crown Princess of Germany, a most zealous supporter of the exhibition, has been fairly earned by the Viscountess Hood for two clever portraits of her children. The Hon. Mabel Hood is a

Figure 1

well-posed and graceful figure, inserted in a square panel in the centre of a willow-pattern plate; the painting is very quiet in tone, and there is a quaintness both in this plate and in the plaque containing the portrait of the Hon. Neville Hood (Fig. 2), which cannot fail to attract attention. There must, we think, have been a strong competition for the chief prize, as the portrait-painting is excellent, and in painter-like qualities Lady Nicholson's charming head of a girl, entitled "Flowers in Winter," leaves little to be desired. Lady Rawlinson sends an admirable portrait of Sir Henry Rawlinson, and a pair of plates the decoration of which is founded upon Persian examples. The ornament has been adapted with great skill, and the beautiful blending of the different shades of blue, so characteristic of Persian work, has been well attained. A "Classical Head," by Mr. Percy Anderson, a swarthy beauty holding a fan, secures the first prize for heads (amateurs).

The flower-paintings constitute, as they always have done, the great strength of the exhibition. We hardly know whether to award the palm to plants treated naturally, or to the many graceful and elegant conventional arrangements of flowers and foliage to be found in the collection. Miss Edith S. Hall has been awarded the Princess Alice prize for her "Daffodil" plate, an example of a simple conventional treatment excellent both in colour and design. Miss Hall has two other plates which are included in the award. Mrs. Bourdin's "Mountain-ash Berries" are well handled, and the "Sunflowers" and "Nasturtiums," by Mrs. G. Stapleton, are boldly and vigorously painted on a dark ground. Messrs. Hancock, of Worcester, have offered a series of prizes, and the chief of them, a five-guinea box of colours, falls to Miss E. Loch for a most beautifully painted "Cardoon Thistle." Nothing could be better than the series of tiles decorated with naturally treated "Lilies," by Miss Ada Beard, who has received for this work and for another study of lilies the silver badge designed and presented by the Princess Christian. There is much freshness and originality in

Figure 2

Figure 3

the work of Mme. Camille Moreau, who for her two plates has been awarded the first prize for ornament (amateur). The former plate, the motive of which is Japanese, is admirable in point of colour, and the other, which represents some little birds quarrelling "under the mistletoe," is cleverly painted. Miss Everett Green groups her birds and flowers very prettily, and for her two plates, "Birds of a Feather flock together" and "Is he Dead?" she has obtained the prize offered by Lady Olive Guinness.

The prizes are divided into two series, so that amateur works may be kept distinct from those by professional artists. There are many reasons in favour of this course, though we should like to see a few prizes thrown open promiscuously to both ranks of competitors, for we can confidently predict that in not a few of the subjects the works of amateurs would fairly hold their own. The first prize for heads by professional artists falls to Miss C.H. Spiers for a well-painted study entitled "Diana Vernon," and the same talented artist has secured the first prize for ornaments for her two plates painted respectively with "Chrysanthemums" and "Hollyhocks." The former subject is admirably handled, and is an excellent example of flower-painting. Perhaps the most successful specimen in this class in the exhibition is a plateau painted with Chrysanthemums by Miss Florence Lewis, which, in addition to gaining her a Princess Alice prize, has been purchased by the Empress of Germany (see our illustration, Fig. 1). The silver medal presented by the Crown Princess of Germany is worthily awarded to Miss Linnie Watt for one of the most charming little pictures in the collection, entitled "Gathering Spring Flowers." It will be remembered that Miss Watt obtained the first prize last year, and her little rustic scenes have a grace peculiarly their own. We have selected this plate for illustration (Fig. 4). The second prize for heads competed for by professional artists falls to Miss Ellen Welby for a well-modelled and expressive portrait on a background of apple blossoms. For perfection of workmanship and complete mastery of her art, Miss Ada Hanbury has few rivals, and the special prize of ten guineas for the best professional work has been awarded to four studies of "Sycamore," "Apple Blossom," "Portugal Laurel," and "Plane," which remind us of the delicate paintings by this lady in last year's exhibition, on which occasion she also secured the special prize. The second prize for ornament goes to Miss Kate Hammond for two plates painted with "Almond Blossoms" and "Jonquils."

The list of prize works is such a lengthy one that the mere enumeration of the awards absorbs the chief part of our space, and, in addition to the prizes, we find a list which occupies three pages of the handy little catalogue containing the names of amateurs and professionals, divided into the three categories of "Very highly commended," "Highly commended," and "Commended," to each of whom a diploma is awarded.

In addition to the works competing for prizes there are a number of paintings of rare merit by foreign artists, and by professionals who do not compete, but whose works support and enhance the efforts of their amateur rivals. Some of these artists are already well known in this country. M. Leonce, who is a large contributor, is a prince among flower-painters; and for the beauty of his portraits and landscapes, M. Clair is a great acquisition to the ranks of the exhibition.

It is somewhat surprising to find how large a proportion of the ladies have attempted portraiture, by far the most difficult branch of art be it remembered; it is not to be wondered therefore, that in the works of this class there are many failures. There are so few animal-paintings in the collection that it is only just to praise the large measure of success attained by Miss E. O. Verner, whose "Tiger's Head" (Fig. 3) has been thought worthy of being commended. The tile-paintings and plaques contain a number of works of great merit, and there are signs that some of our manufacturers are alive to the advantages of art workmanship in ceramic decoration. Many of the tiles are painted with subjects from some of the familiar nursery story-books, and the illustrations of the old nursery rhymes have inspired not a few of the amateur tile-decorators. Miss Isabel Rogers sends some tiles of admirable design.

We find it impossible to mention all the works we had noted, but we must not forget to call attention to the cleverly designed figures by Mr. H. Thomas, the studies of heads by Mrs. Bristowe, the "Pompeian" design by Mr. C. E. Willis, which seems to be founded upon some old Flemish example, and is novel and praiseworthy. A portrait of G. Startin, Esq., by Miss A. Saltmer, is excellently painted. Mrs. Shearman sends a well-executed panel of "The Christian Martyr." The two figure subjects, "Peter Snellinx" and "Helen Fremont," by Miss C. Haucke, are well painted. Among the flower-paintings we noted were Mr. Leonce's "Group of Sunflowers, Pansies, &c.;" "Ox-eye Daisies," by Miss H. S. Bishop; "Chrysanthemums," by Miss G. Swears; and "Dog Roses," a pretty design in blue and white, by Miss M. Voss. Among so many works of great merit it seems invidious, however, to single out thus only one or two for special mention. The collection is full of interest and promise.

Figure 4

A New Lustred Pottery

An article by Professor A.H. Church, describing William De Morgan's early work, which appeared in *The Portfolio* 1876, p.114.

The peculiar brilliancy of polished metals is due to a very intense reflection of the incident light. This reflection constitutes the lustre known as 'metallic,' and consists of pencils of rays which are generally coloured by reason of the selective absorption exercised upon the white light by the illuminated surface. These metallic lustres are produced by other materials in addition to metals. They are seen in the brilliant plumage of humming-birds, the wing-cases of many beetles, and the nacre of certain shells. It is, perhaps, to attempts at imitating some of these natural effects of light that we owe the early examples of the peculiar and often beautiful pottery known as *lustred* ware. In such wares a film of actual metal is not always present, some compound substance, such as a metallic oxide or sulphide, being occasionally the reflecting material. The lustring is effected by one of the processes known to chemists as 'reducing,' and to potters as 'stifling.' If, when the ware has been decorated with ordinary enamel colours and fired, it be again touched with certain easily fusible and reducible metallic preparations, on heating it a second time in the kiln, and introducing a little resin or wood, the fumes of these matters will have the effect of reducing some of the metal, and so forming a thin but lustrous coating on the ware. The process requires knowledge and skill, but is not really dificult. If the traditions of this curious art, with their minute but empirical directions, had not been lost, there would have been nothing to prevent its frequent adoption in the potteries of the present day. But chemical knowledge, and many practical trials, with, we may add, many disappointing failures, can replace or recover tradition. Thus it is that we have to draw attention to a modern reproduction of the ancient lustred wares. Mr. William De Morgan, an artist of considerable power and culture, and doubtless an appreciative admirer of the ancient lustred wares of Persia, Italy, and Spain, has devoted some years of experiment to the recovery of a lost art. In Italy, indeed, such efforts have not been uncommon of late, but they have been directed mainly to a not altogether laudable end, the slavish copying of the examples of the 15th or 16th century. These copies have often been sold, after appropriate chipping and rubbing, as genuine productions of the ancient studios of Gubbio and Pesaro. Other modern attempts at lustre colours, as those of M. Brianchon of Paris, copied at Worcester, and Belleek, are rather thin in effect and are used in too mechanical a way to be satisfactory to the eye.

At present Mr. De Morgan merely decorates the wares manufactured for him in Staffordshire, or the tiles commonly imported from Holland. He has successfully introduced three varieties of lustre, comprised in the *madreperla* of the Italians, or the *reflet métallique* of the French. In one of these kinds, the colour of the decoration, a brownish red, due to copper, reflects in certain positions a brilliant hue, often approaching, and sometimes equalling, the famous ruby lustre of Mo. Giorgio. Another kind, derived from silver, is yellowish grey in colour, but shows a soft azure reflection; while a third sort, of an ochreous hue when seen in the ordinary way, fluctuates in lustre between a golden bronze and the pink of almond-blossoms. Vases, plates, and tiles, are decorated with these lustres, no ordinary enamel colours being used to enhance their effects. The plain ground, creamy or white, of the earthen plate or tile, shows itself here and there, but we confess we should like to see the lustred decoration set off by a deep puce or manganese back-ground, or bordered by a greyish black. But these and other developments of the art will follow, doubtless, in due course. We ought not to forget to commend the broad style of decoration which Mr. De Morgan has adopted. A bold border of conventional leafage, mingled with curious monsters, quaint of wing and intricate with foliated tails incalculably coiled, encloses a central medallion containing a bird, a serpent, a stag, or a ship. The designs are kept flat, and do not distract the attention from the lustre, which is, we assume, the true *raison d'être* of the large pieces. Some of the happiest bits of brilliant reflection are to be found on the backs of the plates, for these have invariably received some strokes from an artistic pencil.

There is a delightful experiment which may be made with these lustred plates (and, indeed, with the ancient examples also). A sheet of white paper is to be fastened to the wall beside a window, and then a piece of the ware is to be so held that the sunlight, streaming in through the window, is reflected from the plate on to the paper: the distance may be varied between one and four or five feet. We now get the lustre in its purity, freed from the local colours of the decoration or the pottery itself. And very beautiful in their hues of violet, and salmon, and amber, and pistachio-green, and rose, are these luminous reflections. It is strange to see the dull earthiness of these wares give rise to such a blaze of colour: perhaps stranger still to mark what innumerable varieties of hue go to make up all this splendour. But the microscope reveals the cause of these fluctuations in colour. We examine with the lens some small speck of lustred surface, say the eye of a bird, and find that, though the general effect of the little spot is azure, yet there is within that disc, one-tenth only of an inch across though it be, a multitude of hues. Outside there is a faint line of bronze; next comes a border of apple-green; and then, in the midst, a surface coloured with turquoise, yet changing and deepening into lapis-lazuli, and mottled with pale violet.

We advise those of our readers who are interested in artistic pottery to pay a visit to 8 Great Cheyne Row, Chelsea, and see for themselves, not only the lustred ware which we have described, but the turquoise and puce vases, and the beautiful enamelled tiles, which Mr. De Morgan turns out of his studio. The ceramic renown which distinguished Chelsea in the eighteenth century will again revive towards the close of the nineteenth.

A.H. CHURCH

William De Morgan

From Reginald Blunt: *The Wonderful Village* (London, 1918), pp. 169-190.

Good fiction survives more housemaids than good pottery, and the name of William De Morgan will doubtless live as the author of "Joseph Vance," "Alice For Short," "Somehow Good," and others of that wonderful succession of novels - which were all produced in the last decade of his life - in the days to come, when his pots and panels are scarcely to be found, save - one hopes and is promised - in South Kensington Museum.

But it is none the less true that it was as a potter and craftsman that the best part of his life was spent, and that it was his work in pottery, alongside of that of William Morris, Walter Crane, and one or two other workers, which laid the foundation for the modern regeneration of the Arts and Crafts, whose first exhibition, in 1888, he helped to organise and beautify.

De Morgan's first labours in stained glass and in pottery were worked out in the later sixties and early seventies at 40 Fitzroy Square, where, as he modestly put it, "his experiments in lustre, at that time not much known in England, attracted some attention among artists"; and where he succeeded in carrying out a good deal of valuable trial work, and incidentally in burning the roof of the house off.

This led to his migration, about 1875, to No. 30 Cheyne Row, Chelsea; whither he moved with his mother and sister, where his small kilns were re-erected in a shed at the end of the back garden, and where - also incidentally - a typical row of his Chelsea tiles may still be seen in the window-boxes.

A few doors above No. 30, at the corner of the Row, stood a spacious old house with a larger garden, known as Orange House, now the site of the Roman Catholic Church of the Holy Redeemer; and this house De Morgan rented for a time from Mr. Wickham Flower as a workshop and showroom, while remaining in residence at No. 30. The coach-house afforded space for a larger kiln; the big first floor rooms housed the leading painters; whilst the ground floor was stocked with the finished work; and De Morgan himself had a room on the second floor, which he used as a studio, and where he also often slept when working late at night. . . .

From Mr. Fred Passenger, who worked as a painter with De Morgan for twenty-eight years, I have recently gleaned a few particulars of the Chelsea days at Orange House, where he began work in 1879, his elder brother Charles having preceded him there by some eighteen months. Ovens were a doubtful addition to the confined areas of Cheyne Row, so the pot and plate and tile designs had to be painted on the most suitable ware that could be procured amongst the potters; but towards the close of the Chelsea period De Morgan, who had never been satisfied with the bought material, began making tiles for himself, getting a crucible clay from the Battersea plumbago works. The kiln at Orange House was built in an old coach-house which stood between the north side of the house itself and Upper Cheyne Row, the flue (with a faith unshaken by Fitzroy Square happenings, and apparently justified this time) being taken into one of the old chimneys of the house. The show-room, with a store-room at the back, occupied the whole ground floor. The decorators, including, beside the two Passengers, Mr. Babb, a young artist, Mrs. Beatty, and Dr. Reginald Thompson, who did some designs of much promise and ability, worked on the first floor, while some half-dozen girls were also employed on Dutch and other tiles, and had a room in one of the Upper Cheyne Row houses. The Chelsea tiles were mostly painted on a red clay body which came from Poole, Dorset; the great dishes and plates for lustre work came from Davis'; and the panels - the beautiful *Livadia* set were made at Chelsea - had to be built up from five and six inch tiles, breaking joints, brick-work fashion, and backed with one or even two thicknesses of plain tile cemented on; the surface being next floated with the white or coloured ground to a more or less even face, and then painted, glazed, and fired as a solid slab. Another difficult and wonderfully successful piece of work which was carried out at Chelsea was the patching and piecing up and completing of the beautiful set of Damascus tiles for the Arab Court of Lord Leighton's house, the texture and colouring of these being reproduced with absolute fidelity.

De Morgan's painters enjoyed their labours at Chelsea, where the workshop was not, as at Merton and Fulham, away from the cheery haunts of humanity, and where the "carriage folk" visiting the showroom below enlivened their window view, and the feeling that one or other of their productions was at that moment finding a purchaser downstairs gave a touch of lively interest and reality to their doings. De Morgan was constantly in and about, working out designs upstairs, counselling and correcting the decorators, meeting friends and visitors below, or superintending the packing of a kiln in the outhouse; and towards evening would often be heard a big voice shouting "Bill!" and footsteps mounting the stairs three at a time like a schoolboy's, which told of the arrival of William Morris with ruffled hair and indigo-stained fingers, keen to discuss some new project or just to hear how things were going with his friend.

Miss May Morris, recounting her recollections of William De Morgan in an interesting paper in the "Burlington Magazine", has given a very pleasant account of the little menage at No. 30, and of the worries and excitements, the depressing failures and triumphant successes of the kiln-firings in Cheyne Row. But no one who has not been actually engaged in fine pottery work can quite realise the strain and tension of the firing of a big pottery kiln, in which, it may be, hundreds of pounds' worth of decorative work, and months of arduous labour, are put to the hazard of the flames; when a whiff of unregulated draught, an ill-secured saggar, a few degrees more or less of furnace temperature, a slight misjudgment of the critical moment of completion - any one of a dozen swiftly changing conditions - may mean all the difference between success and irretrievable disaster. More than once I have been by William De Morgan's side at these supremely critical moments and admired the coolness and quiet resource - the high-pitched voice never quitting its resonant drawl - which masked the excitement of a big issue in the balance. But the end, whatever it was, was sure to reveal the rare good traits, the grit, perseverance, and invincible humour; boyish delight, it may be, in a fine thing finely achieved; at the worst, an object lesson or a clue won and registered, with a smile, from failure.

About 1879, I think, the first of the great series of ship panels was begun for the Czar of Russia's yacht *Livadia,* at Chelsea; and these were succeeded, in later years at Merton and Fulham, by a notable succession of cabin and stateroom decorations for six P & O liners; now, alas, almost without exception sent to the bottom of the oceans by Hun torpedo or other catastrophe.

But, as the orders increased, and as a term of lease sufficient to warrant extensive alterations could not be obtained of Orange House, De Morgan was forced to look about for other and more spacious accommodation. William Morris, who was himself anxious to gather his various industries together at this time, hoped that De Morgan might arrange to join him on the same premises; and together they hunted various neighbourhoods accessible from London, in the hope of discovering the ideal spot. At length, after many disappointments, Morris decided upon Merton Abbey, with the waters of the Wandle for his dyeing troughs; and in 1882 De Morgan also took some land at Merton (although not actually adjoining) and built his kilns and workrooms there, henceforward designing, throwing, and completing his own pots and tiles, and keeping Orange House for a showroom only; till 1886, when the shop in Great Marlborough Street was taken, and the finished work transferred there from Chelsea. But by this time he had settled into residence at The Vale - that secluded little sanctuary off the King's Road just west of Church Street, now alas, no more - and found the daily journeys to and from Merton too much of a trial and waste of precious time; and accordingly, some two years later, he took courage in both hands and began the building of a much larger factory at Sands End, Fulham, the approach to which was christened De Morgan Road. Here, for the remainder of its existence - nearly twenty years - the pottery work was continued. His principal workmen, Iles, the kiln foreman (who was later joined by his son) and the two brothers Passenger followed him from Chelsea to Merton and from Merton to Fulham, and remained with him faithfully to the very end; and his relationship to them revealed, throughout, the ideal - but not easy - standard of craft co-operation between master and men. With the beginning of the Sands End Pottery it was that he took Mr. Halsey Ricardo into partnership; a combination full of promise for vigorous decorative developments.

But three or four years after the establishment of the works at Fulham, William De Morgan's health caused some anxiety, and his doctor thought it necessary to insist that he should winter abroad for the future.

To the satisfactory continuance of most handicraft of so individual a character, such a compulsory severance for half the year would have been rapidly fatal. In any case, it could not but tell against success; but in his, the effect was greatly mitigated by the peculiar process of tile painting so successfully employed by him; in which the designs were painted by hand in pottery colours on a coarse, thin, whitey-brown paper mounted on glass, and afterwards laid down on the white ground of the tile body, which was then coated with glaze, and finally fired; the paper being thus entirely consumed, and the coloured pattern remaining embedded beneath the surface of glass.

This method enabled De Morgan to execute nearly all the tile painting in Florence, which was his winter home, by the hands of clever, quick-witted Italians, under his personal supervision and training, in an ideal workshed in his garden by the Mugnone; the papers being posted in batches to Fulham for laying and firing, and samples of new patterns being sent out on special thin tiles for his inspection and correction.

Meanwhile, his partner was able to look after the general working of the Sands End factory through the winters, and to superintend the showroom business at Great Marlborough Street till 1897, when stress of other work made this more difficult for Mr. Ricardo; and I was invited, for the next three winters, to supervise the doings at De Morgan Road as General Manager and "Chancellor of the Exchequer", under their friendly tutelage. The arrangement helped to make possible the continuance of the factory, though the Chancellor's Treasury suffered from chronic depletion; but the enforced absence of its chief was, of course, a severe handicap. The whole of the making and firing of the tiles and pots, and the decoration of the latter, had naturally to be done at Fulham; as well as the scheming of orders, the building and repairs of kilns and machinery, and the endless minutiae of works management. Correspondence was slow, misunderstandings were occasionally inevitable, and the absence of the guiding and creative spirit of the master could not but be severely felt. Still, with Mr. Ricardo's help and guidance till the end of 1898, when the partnership was dissolved, I did my best to carry on, in the spirit and tradition of the founder; I worked hard at the chemistry of fluxes, grounds, and glazes; I learnt what I could of practical decorative principles under Lewis Day; I studied the odious complexities of book-keeping and got the books and accounts into good working order; I did what could be done to encourage the staff, to prevent jealousy and friction, and to develop the special qualifications of each; and I reported our doings and difficulties fully to Florence every week. For me, at least, it was an experience and an education full of interest and value; and through all its worries and anxieties it was made delightful by De Morgan's unfailing kindness and too generous appreciation of my poor and very amateurish help; and by the charm and patience and all-pervading humour of his long weekly letters.

By Mrs. De Morgan's kindness, I have recently been reading again this substantial budget of correspondence. . . . .

I take passages at random from the pile of letters before me:- "All the misfortunes I have ever met with I have afterwards found I should have avoided if I had relied on my own convictions. I'm afraid I'm almost too old now to profit much by the lesson, but better late than never. . . . I know of a great many quarters that would believe in D.M. & Co. if D.M. was to be kept in a sort of aesthetic pound, and not allowed to meddle with ledgers. . . . I shall catch it . . . . . for delaying the shop with new patterns, - but it is the way to resurrection; and the policy of perpetual repetition, though forced on us temporarily by the unreachability of the retail public, is merely a form of slow death. . . . I have *endless* chemical problems for solution, which I have puzzled at since 1873. The ways in which the copper turquoise varies is one of them . . . . It is years since I tried the comparison, but it would be worth trying again on that very account. The same spooks may not be in the neighbourhood. It's them as upsets one. . . ."

"It is rather melancholy to think any of my men should be conducting omnibuses. What I'm curious to see is if, when any of them come back to my work (if they do) they will be happy, and won't find it dull by comparison. . . . I am hoping to get the chaps here [in Florence] decorative work to do; and this will be a great convenience, because I shall be able to get tile work done when wanted, by special job, and not have to keep them all going always. I wish something of the kind were possible in England; if only the chaps could groce greens, or monge iron, or victual licentiously, while employing odd hours for painting!. . . . ."

"I'm just going to pack and send off a carved wood handle of a pot to mould from; also the profile to cut the zincs from. It is to be an eight faced pot, and we will lustre it when I come back and make it a wunner [*sic*] or *capo d'opera*. . . . The stamped tiles are trials, and must await their own completion to know how large an organ of self-esteem they may safely indulge in. . . . ."

"I imagine that if the floor holds out long enough we will get the big kiln into complete working order and run up the stock of plain tiles to cheapening point, which I look to as to a millennium. Clay in barges of 80 tons from Stourbridge; a mill turning out 5 tons per diem of body; all the rooms full of workers, and 18/- a yard for turquoise tiles; - that's my idea of things. As for there being *no market,* that's simple nonsense. There's the whole wide world, and what can one want more. . . . ."

The following is of interest as explaining why De Morgan insisted on making his tiles, and not merely decorating them:-

"Perhaps I owed you (I think I did) a fuller résumé of the reasons I had for making my own tiles. Well! I'm not the man to begrudge it, and here it is."

"At some date in the early seventies I was struck by the fact that the employment of tiles in European buildings never approached in extent to the use that I have always understood has been made of them in other countries, especially in Persia. This seemed particularly noticeable in external work. In my frequent conversations with architects, I observed that the reason invariably alleged for this last was that tiles would not bear the frost or hold tight on cement or mortar. Observation confirmed this. I also observed that the tiles pointed at as having these defects were always the pressed dust tiles, or Minton tiles, so called because the invention of the press was either Herbert Minton's, or because he bought the patent. In time I came to the conclusion that the artificially compacted clay differed in molecular structure from that of natural shrinkage from the wet."

"It is more absorbent, or rather absorbs with greater capillary attraction (for I doubt the same bulk of pressed tile absorbing as much water as one of ours; but I don't know). Of course, I did not then *know* that tiles I made myself from wet clay *would* stand frost and wet. I only believed it. I have not yet had sufficient experience to speak positively; but, generally speaking, the twenty years that I am just completing seems to point to the accuracy of my first conclusions. I found also that as a matter of economy it did not seem a much greater expense to make my tiles than to buy them. . . . . The advantage of the pressed dust tiles is a purely commercial one; they are so exactly 6ins. x 6ins., and so exactly the same size that a person who has given a heavy order, and changes his mind, cannot bilk the manufacturer on the ground of the goods not answering the description. It *is* an advantage."

This is spoken feelingly, because De Morgan's tiles were apt to vary slightly in size owing to irregular shrinkage of the body; and this lack of deadly uniformity was, in my experience, used as an excuse for returning a consignment in more than one instance.

Contradictory as it sounds, it was, perhaps, to some extent the wide range of William De Morgan's inventive and creative ability which tended in a measure to hamper the success of the pottery. Apart altogether from the creation of designs, his chemical investigations into the qualities and kiln-behaviour of various bodies, calcines, frits, and glazes, and the practical improvements he introduced in the design of ovens and kilns, and the regulation of temperatures and draught, were of course an essential and most valuable part of the work. His revival of the fifteenth century metallic lustres of the great masters of Italian Majolica at Pesaro, Gubbio and Deruta, led to the production of his most characteristic ware; . . . . . But the versatile genius for contrivance and improvements which he inherited from his father was not, as he said, to be impounded, either aesthetically or technically; and was devoted impartially also to the evolution of telegraphic codes, of tile pattern indexes, of systems of accounts, of machinery design, of stock reference lists, and other side issues which poorer brains could have tackled well enough. De Morgan's mind was ever full of original methods and ideas in all sorts of subjects; he invented new processes in glass staining, in glycerine painting, in clay casting, in grinding mills; he devoted endless labour and ingenuity to a pneumatic speed change gear for bicycles; he latterly attacked some of the most difficult problems connected with aircraft and submarine work; he was proud of his descent from a grandfather, William Frend, "who was expelled from Cambridge University for heretical opinions;" and he was always loth to accept preconceived systems of doing things until he had made trial of his own . . . .

As a matter of fact he continued the work at Fulham - largely I think out of consideration for his men - for several years longer; and it was only in 1907 that he decided to stop work there finally. Though other circumstances had their part in this conclusion, it was, I think, essentially a case of slow starvation amidst plenty; the impossibility, that is, through insufficient capital, of organising the output, on a sufficiently large scale, of products for which, at the prices which large production would have made possible, there would have been an ample and regular market. That, however, is controversial ground, on which there is no need to enter further here. "Our poor trade," he wrote to me, "is famished not for want of customers, but stock."

Pity it is - as one must always feel with whatsoever things are lovely and of good report - that the making of William De Morgan's beautiful Chelsea ware has to be numbered amongst the vanished things from among us. Grievous it may be that his dream of dispelling London's architectural gloom by fine masses of richly coloured tile and panel work - of which his partner has given us an appetising glimpse of Mr. Debenham's house in Addison Road, which contains a splendid presentation of De Morgan's best colour work, admirably chosen, and set forth with sympathetic ability - should remain a dream. But there are generally two sides to a profit and loss account; and we must not forget, in debiting Pottery with his art, that we have simultaneously to credit Literature with its gain, and that branch of it which attracts about 90 per cent. of its supporters. For in 1906 "Joseph Vance" appeared, and took the novel-reading world by storm; to be followed annually by that remarkable succession of stories which has endeared the name of De Morgan to thousands who would never otherwise have heard it. The lustred bowls, the glowing pots, the turquoise tiles, beautiful as they were, remained always - though not by his wish - the prizes of the few; the wondrous beasts and birds, the ships, the fishes, and the sea life, the perfectly adapted pattern of sweeping forms of limb and fin and wing, of flower and foliage; the quips of humour, the transparencies of atmosphere, the swirl of wave, the shimmer of watery deeps; all these things of delight which his designs forecast and his pottery, at its rare best, achieved, are a richly imaginative but yet a very limited and precarious heritage.

Lustre Ware

From a paper read by William De Morgan to the Society of Arts and printed in the *Journal of the Society of Arts* 40 (1892), pp. 756-764.

The process of lustre decoration is not described by Brongniart, who was the great technical authority on pottery of fifty years ago; and Salvêtat, who was his successor, makes only a very speculative allusion to its possible character. And in the catalogue of the Great Exhibition of 1851, which is a sort of death register of the arts of antiquity, not a hint of lustred pottery appears. The modern revivals begin with those at the Ginori factory at Doccia, near Florence, and those of Carocci at Gubbio, of which Mr. Fortnum speaks very highly. There were some of these in the 1862 Exhibition in London. I have never seen any myself. The best I have seen are those of Cantagalli, at Florence.

In spite of the Doccia and Gubbio reproductions, an impression continued to prevail that the process was a secret. I used to hear it talked about among artists, about twenty-five years ago, as a sort of potters' philosopher's stone. At that date the attempts to reproduce it in England had met with only very partial success, although an Italian had gone the round of the Staffordshire potteries showing how to do it. Even now it is sometimes spoken of as a secret by newspaper writers. My attention was attracted to some very interesting work of Massier, of Cannes, in the last Paris Exhibition, by a newspaper paragraph headed "Re-discovery of a Lost Art."

In fact, re-discovery appears to have dogged the footsteps of the lustres from the beginning. I re-discovered them myself in 1871, or thereabouts, and in the course of time some of my *employés* left me, and re-discovered them again somewhere else. I do not think any re-discoveries of this sort contributed in any way to the very general diffusion of the process in the potteries at this moment. Very likely some of them have an earlier record than mine, but the only one I chanced upon when I was in Staffordshire was that of the late Mr. Clement Wedgwood, who showed me a number of experiments which would have been successes if the glaze had been suitable, and a small sample shown me by the late Mr. Colin Campbell. As far as the technical difficulties of simply evolving a copper or silver lustre go, I see no reason why (as in the case of the Arabs and Italians) every discovery should not be totally unconnected with every other. But there was one thing the Italians found out, when they reproduced the Moorish firings, namely, how to make a strong, and beautiful, and original use of their materials. It may be that the less we say about the modern parallels of their case the better.

Perhaps we may now make a new departure, and consider that the process is as well known as any other process in the arts; at any rate, I will contribute what I can to make it so, by telling all I know of it myself. I got nothing from Piccolpasso, as I did not see the work till long after, nor from any printed information, except the chemical manuals I had read in youth. The clue was furnished by the yellow stain of silver on glass. When over-fired this shows iridescence, which is often visible on the opaque yellow visible from the outside on stained glass windows. I tried that stain on Dutch tiles, and found them unsusceptible in the glass kiln, but, in a small gas muffle, I found that both copper and silver gave a lustre when the gas was damped down so as to penetrate the muffle. I pursued my investigation, and, after an interruption, occasioned by setting the house on fire and burning the roof off, I developed the process in Chelsea. This was 1873-74, since which time it has not varied materially, although I have tried many experiments, with a view to improving it.

As we now practise it at Fulham, it is as follows: The pigment consists simply of white clay, mixed with copper scale or oxide of silver, in proportions varying according to the strength of colour we desire to get. It is painted on the already fused glaze with water, and enough gum arabic to harden it for handling and make it work easily; a little lamp black, or other colouring matter, makes it pleasanter to work with. I have tried many additions to this pigment, of infusible white earths such as lime, baryta, or strontia, and other metallic oxides, but without superseding the first simple mixture. Any infusible clay will answer the purpose, though we have always used kaolin, as the least fusible. In Deck's work on pottery he gives several receipts for lustre pigments, only one of which seems to me to belong to the true process of lustre. The others all contain sulphur, which is not necessary, though it may work very well. The sulphur lustres are akin to the old Swansea lustre, which only requires to be burnt at a low heat without smoke. The sulphur evaporates and leaves a metallic deposit which is not oxidated, or only partly so, by the access of air after the sulphur vapour has left the kiln. I believe all the lustres included in the colour-maker's lists are of this nature, but the results produced in modern ware do not tempt the investigator. The prettiest one I have seen is Burgos lustre, which, however, contains gold. The only ingredient containing sulphur mentioned by Piccolpasso would be the small quantity of vermilion (that is, if *cinabrio* means vermilion), which he adds to his receipt for *oro*. Piccolpasso's recipes are the diluent clay only, as he says nothing of either copper or silver. But he had them from hearsay, and if he really tried to produce lustre with them without any addition of metal, it quite accounts for no lustres ever appearing at Castel-Durante, where he was master potter. Indeed, it raises the question whether he was not hoaxed by Maestro Cencio, Giorgio's son, who is supposed to have given the information.

The ware, when painted, is packed in a close muffle, which is then raised to a very low red heat, so low, when the ordinary tin enamels are employed, as to be only just visible. A charge of dry wood, sawdust, wood-chips, or, indeed, any combustible free from sulphur, is then introduced into the muffle through an opening level with the floor, a space having been left clear under the ware for its reception. As soon as it has blazed well up, the opening is closed. The flare then chokes down and the combustion of the charge is retarded, the atmosphere in the muffle consisting entirely of reducing smoke. The test pieces will soon begin to show a red or yellow stain, the pigment itself looking black, until it is wiped off to show the stain. This operation must be repeated until the tests look right, when the fires should be drawn and the muffle left to cool.

The difference between this operation and Piccolpasso's is chiefly in the use of the closed muffle, which is rendered necessary by the difference in fuel. The sulphur from coal or coke would injure the glazes where there was no lustre, and would interfere with the process itself. In the Italian process, where wood is the fuel, the wood is packed in a perforated sagger, into which the smoke from the furnace is choked back by closing a damper, or by simply increasing the volume of smoke from the furnace by heaping on brushwood. But the principle of the operation is the same in both cases, and the dangers are the same. The firing may be vitiated in either by any of the following causes. There may be too great heat, or too prolonged heat; the smoke may be too dense, or too attenuated, or not long enough maintained, or the reverse. If more than one of these factors is wrong at the same time, the harm done will be in proportion. Even when the conditions are most closely observed, the results will show unexpected variations. It is impossible to secure uniformity throughout a muffle. Consequently, the size of the ware must be small in proportion to that of the muffle, or a vase might be overdone at the top and underdone at the bottom, while a number of small pots in the same space would have turned out very well, a few of the top ones being uniformly overdone (and perhaps little injured), and a few of the bottom ones underdone, and only wanting a second similar firing. This also makes a longer and slower firing necessary with larger ware, and this means more risk.

The different sorts of copper lustre may be classified thus;—

1. Opaque metallic copper deposited on the surface of the glaze. The oxide is in this case probably reduced at the moment of deposit. Nearly the same result takes place in the common lustre of the potteries, where the sulphur of the sulphide of copper is driven off by a low heat.

2. Combination of copper suboxide with the glaze without reduction to metal. This is to all intents and purposes the same thing as when glass containing copper is flashed and becomes ruby. The harder the glaze is, and the higher the temperature, the less likely is a deposit of metallic copper.

3. The result of prolonging heat without smoke on No. 1. The deposited copper is thus slowly absorbed into the glaze, becoming ultimately red without lustre, but passing through every intermediate stage.

4. The result of increasing the reducing agent on No. 2. In this case the oxide already in combination is brought back to the state of metal. I believe that all the best lustre should be classed with this or No. 3.

Silver lustres show the same results, but at a lower temperature. So when both lustres are fired together, we may expect Nos. 3 and 4 of silver lustre, with Nos. 1 and 2 of copper.

The ugliest results are when the glazes are overcharged to the point of opacity. But accidents of this sort may be taken advantage of when the designer foresees the result. For instance, great blotches of opaque pale yellow on an inky background may be very ugly, when an arabesque of fine lines of the same yellow on the same ground might be rather pretty.

I have said that the tin glaze is the most susceptible to lustre, but it does not necessarily give the finest results. The Gubbio lustres are really on superposed marzacotto, and possibly the exceptional beauty of some Persian lustre may be due to what is often called a siliceous glaze, which is what I call an alkaline glaze, as all glazes are siliceous. A film of such a glaze over the tin would almost elude any possible means of detecting it, and yet would scarcely be penetrated by the lustre colour, so thin is it.

The best of the first lustres I made on Staffordshire ware were on ironstone or granite. The body was repellent in colour, but the glaze particularly good. Latterly, we have used the common opaque white made with tin. It has also been ugly in colour, being, I believe, made so by the addition of cobalt, to make it whiter, just as the house-painter spoils his beautiful white chalk with French blue. I have tried many experiments with glazes, but I am inclined to think that the way they are fired in the glost oven has as much to do with their adaptability for lustre as their chemical composition.

I have also tried in this past 20 years a vast number of experiments, with the idea of adding to the first simple process of the Arabs. To save others needless work, I will enumerate a few, with my recollection of their results.

1. Reduction by other agents than carbonaceous smoke; by ammonia, by steam in contact with reducing fuel, by coal-gas, by vapour of water and glycerine or spirit. None of these gave any new results.

2. The use of copper and silver colours as enamels, or under glaze, and their subsequent reduction by any of these agents. Sometimes there were good results, but the colour was always patchy.

3. The deposit of copper or silver from vapour of the chlorides, ammonium chlorides, or iodides, those portions of the glaze being protected which were to remain white. These experiments might be repeated with advantage. A similar one was the painting of the pattern in a susceptible glaze on a refractory one, and its exposure to vapour containing copper or silver. The suboxide of copper itself vaporises under certain conditions, which is the cause of the flown red colour occurring on many examples.

I have, of course, tried endless modifications of the ordinary process, such as using special woods for smoking. sawdust, shavings, paraffin, and other combustibles. Any of these answer the purpose, the application being slightly varied. But nothing material has come of any of these experiments, and the process remains substantially the same as at first. I believe that if there had been any new opening for the application of chemistry, although I might not have followed the clue successfully, I could hardly have missed it altogether.

In conclusion, I may say that I believe we have learned all there is to know of the chemical and mechanical side of the art, as it was known to the ancients. What remains to be discovered in order to produce original work, equal to that of the Renaissance, is not a technical mystery, but the secret of the spirit which animated the 15th century not only in Italy, but all through Europe. We have got the materials and many more, but the same causes that forbid the attainment of new beauty with the new ones, have stood between us and the revival of old beauty with the old. In saying this, I do not suppose myself to be going outside a universally accepted truth, or, at any rate, one that is very rarely questioned. Some day there may be a new imagery and a new art. In the meanwhile I can only say that if anyone sees his way to using the materials to good purpose, my experience, which I regard as an entirely chemical and mechanical one, is quite at his disposal.

The "Della Robbia" Pottery Industry

An anonymous article which appeared in the *Magazine of Art*, XX(1896), pp. 6 — 8.

A new industry has been established at Birkenhead of so distinctly artistic a nature that it is with pleasure we call attention to it. The first object of its promoters, Mr. Harold Rathbone and Mr. Conrad Dressler, was the revival of a modelled glazed or enamelled earthenware with coloured grounds for purposes of architectural decoration after the manner of the *faïence* of the great Italian family of Della Robbias, who flourished in Florence at the time of the Renaissance. The introduction into architectural schemes of bands or accents of rich colour which would still withstand the effects of the English climate in external as well as internal ornamentation would be of supreme value in lightening up the rather sullen and smoky buildings of our great cities. It has already been proved to some extent what a telling effect the tiling to window garden boxes imparts to

many of the large mansions which otherwise possess such an extraordinary similarity, and this practice might be very considerably developed with a constant variety of design and colour which would be a source of pleasure to the passers-by and those who inhabit the neighbourhood. Friezes with figure or floral design, or panels in low relief let into the ordinary white tiling with simple bands of green or red colour, might be made considerable use of. Fountains in this material might also be introduced into some of the new restaurants or large hotels, and add a character of charm and entertainment like one is aware of in the foreign cities. This use of enamelled earthenware is certainly more suitable than the structural use, as a surface that is glassy is apt to give one a certain want of confidence as to its service of strength and permanence. The setting-in of tiling, say, blue and white, into the woodwork of an overmantel, or the introduction of tall panels in the side pilasters, form other legitimate uses of this material, and would supply a valuable note of colour to continue the same scheme of decoration in the draperies and wall hangings, or some treatment which would equally well harmonise with the blue and white. Together with the architectural works has been carried on a pottery for the production of fine shapes and colours with a good deal of work in the *sgraffito* treatment on the model of the old Italian workers — with designs occasionally taken from the old ones in order to keep the standard of designing as high as possible, but more often invented by the pupils, whom it is the object of the working manager to see how far he can let alone — in order to bring out — the full fancy and originality of each individual worker; though every care is taken that the best principles of design are preserved as well as may be. It was the object thus to make the articles in everyday use comely and entertaining in shape, design and colour treatment, so that thus the ordinary meal would have the comparative air of a banquet like those beautiful dishes that one sees in the pictures of banquets by Sandro Botticelli and others, where, as in the feast of Peleus by our own Sir Edward Burne-Jones, the sense of beauty is appealed to, and one is made aware how lovely is the fruit itself. Marmalade pots (with a hole for the spoon) and porridge plates, egg stands and muffin dishes, and milk and water jugs, are amongst these useful articles, not to mention the rose bowls and inkstands for the use of the boudoir. Nothing could be prettier than a dessert service in this *sgraffito* treatment, and it is a source of grief to the manager that the ware is used so much more freely for merely decorative purposes than for absolute daily use. One of the last letters written by Lord Leighton, P.R.A., was in reference to the Della Robbia pottery, and dwelt very much on this principle. He wrote:- "I have learned with great satisfaction that you do not confine

yourself to the production of pieces destined wholly for decoration, but have grasped the vital principle that the chief object of a manufacture of this kind must be, if it is to thrive, the application of artistic qualities to objects of ordinary domestic use. It was this principle which gave to the work of the Greeks in ancient days, and to that of other European nations in the Middle Ages, that distinction and beauty which are our envy and admiration to this day."

Employment is found at the Birkenhead Potteries for many young people of both sexes who show artistic taste, and, in curious contradistinction to Mr. Herkomer's statement at the Eistedfodd last summer, it is found that those with the most highly gifted colour sense are of Celtic origin from the north of Wales. The best of their colourists is Miss Hannah Jones, who has undoubtedly influenced the work of the other girls at the Pottery. There is, too, a Welsh boy employed who never had a drawing lesson in his life, but who took the gold cross for originality of design in pottery at the Home Arts and Industries Exhibition last year. This lad is also clever at throwing, handling, and modelling; and is at present employed dipping the red clay vessels into the white slip. Another designer of striking originality is Miss A. Pierce, whose sister, Miss Lena Pierce, produced some beautiful and romantic designs before her early death.

There is reproduced on this page a design of a "Guardian Angel," by Miss Ropes, of London, whose work is found to be peculiarly adaptable to Della Robbia methods. Mr. Anning Bell and Mr. Charles Allen, at the Liverpool College, are producing pupils whose work promises well for future use. It is hoped to extend the work for architectural purposes.

At present two panels have been placed on a private house in Liverpool, representing a sower and a reaper; and an angel — which is reproduced — for a lunette at the house of Mr. Walter Holland. In the Town Hall at Liverpool, on one of the mantelpieces, is a large vase, designed by Mr. Harold Rathbone, flanked by a pair of vases modelled on the lines of the old Pilgrim vases at South Kensington. Beside these an ingle-nook has been executed for Lord Radnor's house at Folkestone.

The "mark" of the pottery is a ship with "D.R." on either side, signifying that the work is produced at a seaport town.

The Watcombe Terra-Cotta Company

An article by Professor T.C. Archer which appeared in the *Art Journal*, 1878, p.172.

Few persons can have failed to notice, in the shops of dealers in the choicer kinds of ceramic wares, during the last seven or eight years, very beautiful specimens in red terra-cotta, remarkable both for the softness and purity of colour, resembling nearly the antique Samian, and for the very classical forms of the utensils and perfect modelling of the parts not thrown or turned. These are the products of a new industry which owes its existence to a pure accident. G.J. Allen, Esq., a former Master of Dulwich College, has erected a handsome mansion, "Watcombe House," in the picturesque *combe*, or vale, of Watcombe, and whilst the labourers were digging out the trenches for the foundations, he was much struck with the peculiarly unctuous nature of the clay they threw out; and under the impression that it was of an unusual character, he took samples to the potteries of Bovey Tracey, Worcester, and Staffordshire, and obtained opinions after experiments with them, which convinced him that the clay was a valuable, and, in this country, unique, pottery clay.

Geologically speaking, the formation from which this peculiar clay is derived is the Triassic, the towering red cliffs of which shut in this lovely vale all around, except on the sea side, or rather end, for it runs inland from the sea like a dried-up fiord. Watcombe House is beautifully situated on the south side of the combe, or vale, and perhaps above or close to the outcrop of the red clay; from it the vale descends considerably, and in its lowest depth the clay pits are found in the middle of a small field. Here the clay is weathered and prepared for the potteries, which are not far distant. Mr. Allen formed a company of seven gentlemen, who elected him chairman, and their idea seems to have been to develop the resources of the neighbourhood rather than personal profit. They were convinced they had on the spot a most beautiful material, and they did not like that it should be unutilised. Every one who has had to do with potteries knows well what this means. If pecuniary results were alone aimed at, the question would be how much cheap and every-day stuff can be turned out. The chairman of this company and his colleagues were, however, gentlemen of taste, and preferred credit to their neighbourhood and its beautiful surroundings before personal gain, and from the beginning this singular establishment went in for the production of fine classical forms, and when figure modelling was taken up, the best modellers who could be procured were employed, and some very beautiful results have been obtained. One of the most noticeable has arisen from the ease with which the clay can be diluted, and its vivid red colour toned by the admixture of lighter clays into exquisitely delicate tints, which produce soft, agreeable effects, where as skilfully employed as it is at the Watcombe Works. The productions of this establishment have been received with great favour in this country, and also abroad, and are shipped in considerable quantities to America and Australia. Wherever they go they will do good, for they are always in good taste, and that in spite of their cheapness, which is remarkable. The great success which this pottery has achieved is without doubt due to the twofold qualities of the present manager, Mr. Brock, who with an excellent appreciation of the beautiful is a good working potter, and succeeds in producing work that pays and pleases as well. No pottery, however well established, can afford to despise pecuniary results, and it is well when the aesthetical can be so far mixed up with that view of the question, or occasionally brought in, as to prove we are advancing in that direction. At the Watcombe Terra-Cotta Works, we have already said, besides the purest classical forms and very artistic figure modelling, some strikingly pretty specimens of painting in coloured clays on the terra-cotta surface have been lately executed, and one large painted plaque we have seen from these works, in coloured clays, is worthy of a place in any important collection. It is quite clear that the good taste shown in these works will produce good results; even in the ordinary wares, especially those glazed like the Japanese, there is a simple prettiness which is certain to be appreciated, and as they are very cheap their diffusion will conduce to improved taste amongst those who use them. The last effort from an Art point of view made at the Watcombe Terra-Cotta Works is a kind of fresco painting on plaques of this beautiful clay. This is the invention of the manager, Mr. Charles Brock, and consists of painting on unburnt tiles with coloured slips, which are partially absorbed into the body and are, of course, imperishably fixed by burning. The originators of this interesting pottery are to be congratulated upon their great success, but still more upon their judgment in selecting the persons best qualified to work the manufacture successfully.

Barum Ware

An article 'from a correspondent' which appeared in *The Artist,* II (1881), p. 212.

Not very long ago, as a well-known connoisseur in decorative art, Mr. C.W. Davis, was strolling down one of the picturesque streets of Barnstaple (of which "Barum" is the early English name), some specimens of quaint pottery caught his eye. At once perceiving the genius and originality they displayed, he made enquiries and found the maker, Mr. C.H. Brannam, was the owner of a small local pottery, and late a pupil of the Barnstaple School of Art. Besides being possessed of artistic feeling and industry, Mr. Brannam was found to be a man of sufficient modesty to accept hints; the "Barum ware" has been developed, and some of the results may now be seen in the galleries of Messrs. Howell & James. Mr. Brannam's early specimens are quaintly shaped jars, &c., of rich red body coated with creamy white slip, the incised patterns showing the red ground, the general effect old-fashioned and charming. Under the valuable suggestions of the gentleman already alluded to the ware has grown bolder in shape, and the glaze, in ruddy browns, rich greens, and a cool celadon grey, is in itself a delight to the artistic beholder. The price of Barum ware is, so far, extremely moderate. I purchased a large jardiniere, with a beautiful incised pattern of conventional orange trees, griffins, &c., for 30s.; some lovely tall jars, "the very thing" for the top of a corner cupboard, were 18s., while smaller specimens were only 7s. or 8s. This ware has met with distinct approval from no less a judge than Professor Church of the Royal Academy, who in one of his recent lectures brought it before the notice of his audience with these words, "The productions of this old Barnstaple pot work stand quite alone in material, decoration, and manner of their execution. This Barum ware reminds one at once of the rare Italian Sgraffiato ware, and some of the quaintest English work of the 17th century. Mr. Brannam designs, makes, decorates, and signs each piece with his own hand."

'SABRETASCHE'.

Elton Ware

An article written by Cosmo Monkhouse, which appeared in the *Magazine of Art*, VI (1882), pp. 228 - 233.

An excellent writer on decorative art has recently made an epigrammatic distinction between himself and other writers. He says of his essays that they originated in his having something to say about his art, instead of having to say something. Mr. Elton, of Clevedon, might differentiate between his pottery and that of other makers in similar terms. His introduction into the world may have been for greater purposes than the manufacture and decoration of earthenware; but there is no doubt that among the things he was designed to do was to show us something new in the way of pottery.

At all events it is certain that he need not have turned his attention to this branch of art and manufacture if he had not been so inclined. Although no one would guess it from his later successes, he is an amateur without training, one of those persons — usually, but very wrongly, deemed so happy — who could be idle if they chose. But he has not chosen to enjoy this privilege, and is probably none the unhappier. He had, as a matter of course, an early bias towards art, which was not without some slight cultivation; but in decoration he has had no teacher, and in the handicraft of pottery his own wits have been his only guide. With one slight exception, no one but those instructed by himself have ever done a stroke of work at the Sunflower Pottery; and his most valuable assistance has been afforded by one clever boy, now a clever young man, of the name of Masters, who has developed under his guidance into a very able potter. Nevertheless the nephew of Sir Arthur Elton has within a few years discovered how to mix clays and glazes, how to build kilns, and to bake a pottery of unusual hardness. His decoration, as we shall see presently, is remarkable both for its taste and originality; but his rapid untaught mastery of technical difficulties is more remarkable still.

Rapid and satisfactory though it has been, his history is a succession of disasters; but English potters, like English seamen, do not know when they are beaten, and Mr. Elton has turned all his mischances into victories. To a reader of his diary — with extracts from which he has been good enough to supply me — the reasons for his perseverance are not easy to discover; but the logic of genius is difficult to formulate, and often the only proof of its existence is its success. At present he has attempted earthenware only, made of brown or reddish clay covered with a coloured coating of similar clay ground very fine and worked up with water to the consistency of cream. This is technically called "slip." A stiffer slip is used for decoration. There is little fundamental difference between Elton, Barum, Vallauris, Linthorpe, Dunmore, and innumerable other wares. In the last three of the particular potteries mentioned the colouring matter in contained in the glaze, and slips are not used for ground-colour. Mr. Elton's glaze, on the other hand, though similar in material, being what is called a "lead" glaze, is always colourless. This is a peculiarity, but it belongs nevertheless to a very 'common class of pottery: — not terra-cotta, which is "soft" but unglazed; not stoneware, which whether glazed or not is fired at a higher temperature and called "hard"; but soft glazed earthenware. Yet, though Mr. Elton has only tried a description of pottery which all the potters of the world have made for centuries, and though he is only a novice at it, he makes it better in some respects than any I know. From certain very simple experiments I have made with a few fragments of his ware and a hammer, it appears to me to be harder to break and to be closer in texture than other modern pottery of the same class. His glaze, too, seems harder than ordinary lead glaze, difficult to scratch, and not liable to "craze" (or crack) in firing. This is a most important quality, as soft earthenware is always, or nearly always, porous, and the use of the glaze in making it water-tight is destroyed if the glaze cracks. You may leave Mr. Elton's vases full of water on a bare table without any fear of spoiling the polish, and they will stand any ordinary collision without fracture. Readers may remember that in my article on Vallauris I mentioned the difficulty which M. Clément Massier had found in discovering a glaze to suit his new "paste" — a glaze which would unite with it properly without cracking. A good glaze is one that will fuse at the right time; and this of course depends upon the heat which the "paste" which it covers requires to be properly baked. It must also expand and contract with the "paste", or else it will assuredly crack like a skin too tight or too loose. That Mr. Elton has obtained a superior paste and a suitable glaze is a sign that he has served his apprenticeship, and is entitled to rank with craftsmen.

It was only in December, 1879, that he first thought of turning his attention to art-work in baked clay. Watching men making tiles in a brick-field, the notion occurred to him of making clay mosaics to be coloured and glazed for the decoration of church walls. He took home some unburnt tiles, cut them up, and, much to his satisfaction, completed a medallion of Sir Philip Sidney. In the simplicity of his ignorance he thought he had only to colour and glaze his clay mosaics and bake them in an open kiln, like a brick-kiln on a small scale, and the trick would be done. He accordingly built such a kiln, and tried. The result was, in his own words, "a dead failure." He built another kiln, with the same consequences. He then thought of an iron glass-painter's kiln; but on calculating the heat he required, and finding he could not obtain it in this sort of kiln, he gave up the idea, and began making experiments in glazes. These he had fired for him in Bristol; and they all failed. His next experiment was to construct a small kiln at home, after the likeness of one he had seen at Bristol. This seems to have been the beginning of his success. It is true that his first firing spoilt everything he put into the kiln, but it showed him that he had found a good glaze. After another failure — which, however, confirmed his faith in the glaze — he thought he would try pottery as well as mosaic; and, not being able to throw on the wheel, he called in the aid of a flower-pot maker. A few things roughly made by this artist, and decorated by

himself as roughly, together with some large mosaics of saints, were his next offering to the Fire god, who, as usual, treated them as mere fuel. The ruin of another batch of pottery by chalkstones breaking through the glaze shortly after it came out of the kiln, revealed the fact that there was something the matter with his paste. This appears to have given him pause; and before he made his next effort he bought some ready-baked and glazed plates, painted them, and fired them in his kiln. This may be said to be the end of his first chapter of accidents. Out of it he got some valuable knowledge, especially as to the depth of his ignorance; while in the way of achievement there was the kiln made and a glaze found.

It was at this period that Mr. Elton hit upon the idea which has given the special character to his pottery. This was to make use of and develop the old plan of decorating by slip, and slip only. But he was still far from its realisation. By the 12th of June, 1880, when he went to Scotland for a holiday, he had not got a clay free from chalkstones; he still relied mainly on the Flower-Pot Man for his shapes; in firing he had had a few successes, but more failures; and his kiln had proved so inefficient that he had determined to pull it down, and build another on a better principle. The next new kiln was even less successful at first — partly on account of the coke which he used in firing; but after having several batches spoilt with sulphur, he abandoned coke, and had a grand success in October, 1880. He soon afterwards grew discontented with his shapes, and determined to teach himself every branch of the manufacture. He set up a potter's wheel on his own premises and practised at it every day; he made numerous experiments in colour; and he altogether succeeded so well that about April, 1881, his "Sunflower" ware became an article of commerce at Bristol, and shortly afterwards in London.

The Flower-Pot Man was now dismissed, and Mr. Elton's only assistant was George Masters, who daily became more useful. But the ware was still very inferior in quality: the glaze "crazing" and the material being porous. The young potter had struck into the right path, but he was not by any means out of the wood. His diary records the peeling of glaze and slip, the sticking of the pieces of pottery to the supports in the kiln and to each other, and the destruction of colour by the high temperature of the kiln. Till about the middle of June, 1882, successes and difficulties alternated, but the diary also records researches and discoveries. Instead of burning his goods once only (clay, slip, and glaze all together), he adopted two firings. He discovered a simple but original contrivance for applying the slip to the body while still very moist, by which he not only saved time but secured more perfect cohesion. He invented several other useful mechanical "dodges"; and gradually, by repeated experiments with clays, and by raising his temperature, he approached his present non-porous body.

In June, 1882, kilns on a plan suggested by all his disasters were finished, but he was again doomed to disappointment. This was not a twelvemonth ago, and all his ingenuity in altering and patching the fine new kilns ended in utter failure. He had to rebuild, alter, divide, and pull down, and it was not until October last that the "Sunflower Pottery" was in full working order again. Now he has a kiln which seems to be absolutely under control, and with an even heat in all its parts. His failures and discouragements have been many and serious. But considering that three years ago he was absolutely ignorant of his craft, and that now, without any regular training but that of experience, he is completely master of it, as well as the possessor of valuable secrets of his own, his success - both with regard to the measure of it and the time he has taken to achieve it - is probably unique in the history of pottery.

I have spoken of Mr. Elton as having had no regular training; it may be well to state clearly a few facts of his life. Born in 1846, he was educated at Bradfield College, near Reading, went to Jesus College, Cambridge, and then, his bent being scientific, to Cirencester Agricultural College. Here he had the benefit of lectures from Professor Church, the celebrated chemist, who in the pages of a contemporary has recently published an interesting article on his old pupil's work. Then he married and settled at Clevedon, and to employ his leisure sat down to mechanics and art-work of various kinds. His father, the late Edmund W. Elton, was no mean artist; and his own (perhaps hereditary) talent for art found exercise in painting on china, in designing furniture, and in wood-carving without instruction from any one. All this amateur art and science was useful to him when he turned his attention to pottery. With the exception of visits to some small potteries where all he learnt was "picked up" without teaching, and a few lessons in throwing from the Flower-Pot Man of my story, he has had no help in learning his craft. His kiln, slip-kiln, drying arrangements, wheel, studio, &c., have been constructed from his own designs without any skilled labour; and with the exception of Masters and the Flower-Pot Man he has employed no one in potting, except boys from the village school, who have received their instruction from him.

What follows is a short description of the process now employed at the Sunflower Pottery. The clay or paste is prepared, and the pieces are "thrown" in the usual way. When

they are dry enough, the sketch of the decoration is deeply incised with ordinary modeller's tools. As soon as the clay is a little drier, slip of the requisite ground-colour is applied all over. After another period of drying, the spaces within the sketched outlines are filled in with very stiff clay. For example, if the outline is a flower's, the leaves and petals are filled in with appropriately coloured stiff slips: red lumps for the flower of a rose, and green lumps for the leaves. Then comes a fourth period of drying, after which the lumps are shaped in low relief according to the decorator's taste. Then the piece is slightly fired - to fix the colour only. It is then glazed, then fired again, and this time to the highest heat it will bear. The ware at present is stacked on shelves in the kiln without "saggers." The chief peculiarities of the process are the application of the slip coating while the pieces are still very moist, the reserve of the hardening firing till all the decoration is complete, and the heat of this final firing, which is greater than that usually applied to pottery of the same class.

There are only two ways of decorating pottery — by slip, or by painting with coloured enamels. *Pâte sur pâte,* barbotine, impasto, are only so many different ways of employing slip, or the paste itself, for decoration. Wedgwood's beautiful Jasper Ware is an instance of its application to stoneware; and on M.Solon's admirable low-reliefs we find it adopted for porcelain. Both in Wedgwood and Solon Ware the decoration principally consists of figures modelled in white slip on paste of another colour. Barbotine is the French workmen's name for the surplus clay which adheres to the fingers in "throwing," and is wiped off from one hand by the other and deposited in a little heap. In the "impasto" work the colours are mixed with diluted clay or "slip" and the decoration is applied with a brush. In some of the so-called barbotine work, the brush is employed; in some, modelling tools. Mr. Elton's process is a mixture of *sgraffito,* or scratched work, and modelled slip. Its peculiarity is, that all the slips are coloured, laid on stiff and rough, and then modelled. The nearest approach to it which I have seen is some rough pottery made, I believe, in Belgium. A teapot given me some years ago has a brown-red ground on which is modelled flatly a root of primroses - the leaves in green, and the flowers in yellow, slip. This is the description and style of decoration that Mr. Elton has carried further than any one else - that is, further in the right direction. I fear that the modellers of those wonderful lilies and roses and shells and frogs and cactuses which we now see sprawling over plates and vases, think that they have carried the art of slip decoration further; and so they have, but it is not in the right direction. This "decoration" is not, properly speaking, decoration at all. It hides and renders useless, even when it does not make hideous, the thing it pretends to decorate.

The success which has attended Mr. Elton in his essays in decoration is no doubt due in great part to a natural gift. But it is also due to his allowing this gift to be restrained by the temper of his materials and tools and the requirements of the occasion. He has not sought to impose upon his ware any preconceived ideas of decoration gathered from other branches of art, nor has he attempted to compass with a bit of wood and clay effects which can only be

attained by the use of a brush and pigments. He has allowed his hand to be guided by the shape of the vessel, and his forms and colours to be determined by the inspiration of the moment. "Sufficient unto the day is the decoration thereof" may be said to have been his motto, in practice if not in principle. His designs, though always strictly regulated by the nature of his means of expression, are never without the fresh charm of improvisation. His productions are, therefore, always homogeneous, however many processes may have contributed to their completion, and their total effect is one of spontaneity. He began, as he says, like an ancient Briton - with roughly moulded vessels and rude instruments. His clay was coarse, and his decoration also. Both have since progressed greatly, but *pari passu,* with much of natural development and brotherly sympathy. He has thus never fallen into either of the two extremes of error which are characteristic of much modern work of the same family - inappropriateness and excess. For whatever is decorated, a simple earthenware vessel or a beautiful woman, the first principles are the same, and are neatly summed up in the words - fitness and moderation.

That Mr. Elton's decoration has these qualities will be apparent even from our woodcuts. From them we cannot, indeed, see how well his colours agree with one another: not only on account of their artistic arrangement, but from a certain oneness of quality for which the language has no name, producing a harmony not only of tint but of tone. But they at least will show that in each piece the beauty of the ornament is entirely subject to the character, and only exists as applied to that particular vessel. Without adaptation the design could not be transferred successfully to another object, however well it looks where it is. In the right understanding of what may be called the "adjective" character of true decoration Mr. Elton is almost an Oriental. He is also one in his gift of what is called conventionalising natural forms. Yet he is thoroughly modern and English withal, taking his suggestions from the flowers and animals he knows, and treating them with a freedom which is only limited by his personal taste, I am afraid that neither his fauna nor his flora have any exact counterparts in the world of nature; but they are admirably suited to the artificial world of decoration, for they possess enough of the beauty and vitality and variety of the things we know to satisfy the desire for recognition, without suggesting comparisons which can only end in disappointment.

One distinctive quality of Mr. Elton's decoration is its freedom, and another is its boldness. The scale of it is always as large as the piece will bear; the detail is generally confined to the emphasis of structure and character. He, however, takes advantage of the capacity of his materials whenever they lend themselves to the expression of truth, though he never forces them into unwilling service. He will, for instance, by a little clever manipulation, make his yellow enamel indicate the roughness and consistency of a lemon, but he will not aim at the delicacy and transparency of a petal. In every case - notwithstanding the ingenuity and resource which may be displayed in particulars - the general effect is never hindered by the elaboration of parts, and the decoration is always dominated by the thing itself, whether it be jug or vase or long-necked bottle. A rude luxuriance, varied occasionally by some quaint or grotesque fancy, is at present the character of Elton Ware, but this has been settled by the material rather than by the artist. All he has done at present should be looked upon as little more than tentative - the production of a genuine artistic faculty working under the limits imposed by an imperfect medium of expression. As far, however, as he and his ware have gone, their progress has been singularly right.

Elton Ware is already useful; it is also artistic in the true sense of that much-abused word. What the Elton Ware of the future may be no man can say; for not a batch is turned out of the Sunflower Pottery which does not show advance and freshness of one sort or another. Lately (since the pieces we have engraved were potted) it has produced new things both in

colour and shape. In the former Mr. Elton has shown originality as well as taste. He has discovered more than one colour which it would be difficult to match. In particular I may mention reds of various tints - from pinky chocolate to a bright anchovy colour; and crimsons and purples of great force. In some of his "splashed" pieces, the reds and blues and greys combine into harmonies which, in their depth and softness, remind one of the *flambé* vases of the Chinese. He has been also very successful with similar blendings of red and purple, red and green, grey and violet; indeed some of his recent work seems carved out of blood-stone or of porphyry. He complains, like all potters, of the difficulty of yellow, but he has more than once succeeded in introducing it with good effect.

In regard to shape, as in other matters, Mr. Elton has not allowed his ambition to outstrip his skill, and his forms have hitherto been characterised by simplicity and quaintness rather than elegance or beauty. In this respect much improvement has been made of late, and more may be expected. In the shallow bowl in our plate called "Bowls and Jars", and in some of the bottles figured in our woodcut of "Pieces with Plain Lips", the somewhat archaic character of his early efforts has been changed for a more graceful style. Here, a few touches of finger and thumb have sufficed to break the monotony of a plain lip; there, pressure applied to both sides has given a double-barrelled character to a neck. Both these simple devices are shown in our illustration of "Pieces with Shaped Lips". The effective quality of Mr. Elton's simple "scratched" decoration may be seen in one of the jugs we have engraved; while another has a quaint snake handle. The pieces represented by themselves have been selected to show the special character of his decoration, which concerns itself principally with flowers and reptiles, though now and then an insect is aptly introduced *more Japonico*. Mr. Elton, I may add, is rather fond of snakes, which, in their pliability of form, lend themselves easily to keramic decoration, and which he uses with singular success and skill.

Elton Ware

A lecture given by Sir Edmund Elton to the Somersetshire Archaeological and Natural History Society and printed in its *Proceedings,* LVI (1910), Part II, pp. 31 - 37.

The beginnings of "Elton Ware" date from about the year 1880, and were on this wise. At the date mentioned I was blankly ignorant of ceramics, though more or less interested in arts and manufacture. This led me one day to the brick-fields where tile-making was in progress, and as I watched, an idea came into my mind, why not make a sort of mosaic in large pieces to be coloured, glazed, and fixed to walls with cement. This method suggested itself as being capable of supplying an effective and inexpensive form of decoration (I had not then seen it done, though it has been made use of with good effect since that time). No sooner was the idea conceived in my mind than I determined to embark on practical experiment, and with this object in view, some tiles in the green state were sent up to my house at Firwood, Clevedon, where I executed a half-length figure of Sir Philip Sidney, taken from some painted glass at Clevedon Court. The work was done in coloured clay of three shades: then with the courage born of ignorance I proceeded to the burning, with no better appliance than a disused greenhouse furnace, altered for the purpose according to my crude ideas. The result, as may be expected, was a total failure.

I will not weary the reader with details of puerile attempts at kiln-building; suffice it to say that failure only seemed to stimulate the desire to carry out the inspiration which had come upon me in the brick-fields.

By the courtesy of the then manager of Messrs. Pountney's, Victoria Pottery, Bristol, I was allowed to see and measure a small experimental enamelling kiln, and I also got from the same source raw colours, and some glaze to practise with. On my return home, with the aid of the local bricklayer, I built a little kiln something like the one in Bristol, and in a comparatively short time I succeeded in obtaining some fairly good results. It was about this time, late in 1880, that a lad named George Masters came into my employ straight from school, who was destined to play a large part in the subsequent development of "Elton Ware". He began by occasionally helping me, and I found him such an interested and efficient helper, that he soon became a permanent worker with me. As time passed on, others came and went, doing more or less useful work, but George Masters still works, with enthusiasm hard to beat, in the production of "Elton Ware" in 1910 as he did in 1880, and is my valued friend and fellow-worker.

The next ceramic attempt was a three-quarter mosaic panel in drab, black and yellow, on a bluish-green dispersed ground, representing St. Stephen. This figure was subsequently exhibited; but the making of mosaic was for various reasons not long continued.

Modern pottery, with few exceptions, was rather unsatisfactory. Why not go back to the earliest beginnings of the potter's art? In this way it seemed probable that something with peculiar characteristics would develop. However, it was all very well to dream of a new pottery, but how were suitable forms to be obtained? There was the primitive thumb and finger work with incised decoration, such as are found in pre-historic burial-places; there were the various methods of casting, and there was the potter's wheel. A first start was made by the aid of a thrower of flower-pots, and rough shapes were produced. I used to stand by as the piece grew under the thrower's hand, and say, "Stop now, bulge out there, draw in here," and so on, till something satisfactory appeared. Then as to decoration, coloured clay slips and lead glazes of various kinds were tried, and other methods were attempted, but finally coloured slip-work was decided upon as the line upon which the infant pottery should proceed.

As time went on, it became evident that if I wished to do anything worth doing I must make myself proficient on the wheel and throw the shapes myself. Even the wheel would have to be of primitive construction, and I decided to use one where the thrower sits on a cross-bar and kicks a lever, which gives the required rotation. The next thing was to procure a wheel — this had to be home-made; so with the aid of the estate carpenter and the local blacksmith one was set up, and every morning I practised on it, till, in a comparatively short time, my desire was attained, and I could myself produce the shapes required. I may add that George Masters soon acquired a like proficiency, more and more faithfully translated my ideas, till practically he took my place at the wheel, and that his work as a thrower is now of the best.

To give some idea of the difficulties which had to be overcome, perhaps a few quotations from my diary may not be out of place.

July 15, 1880. — "Built new kiln and prepared 248 experiments; kiln gave way; shelves were broken; all experiments spoilt."

"Pulled down and rebuilt kiln; fired 58 experiments; sulphur came in and experiments were damaged, but results were a trifle better."

"About August 25 fired 86 experiments with wood fuel; everything spoilt but two pieces."

August 2. — "Tried salt glazing; result a failure."

This sort of thing went on with aggravating sameness, but the advance was steady. In the early part of 1881 a batch was spoilt through minute particles of lime. This necessitated the construction of a slip-kiln for the preparation of the body. The kiln was a success, but it was far from being straight sailing; mishaps followed at intervals, but before the end of the year the production of a sound and marketable ware was an accomplished fact.

The general lines of the process in those early days for the coloured ware was as follows — though many changes in detail have been made, and disasters from various causes have not been unfrequent. The body of "Elton Ware" was then, as now, principally formed of the ordinary red brick-clay of the district, mixed with white, or with Rockinham. The method of manufacture differs little from that used by our Somerset forefathers in forming their pitchers and posset-cups, which are found in the neighbourhood today. First the clays are mixed with water to about the consistency of cream, and then passed through fine sieves of wire-lawn, after which the moisture is driven off by heat, dug out, and beaten together till the mass is homogeneous. It is now ready for the thrower. The piece to be decorated is formed entirely on the wheel, and subsequently handled or spouted and finished by hand, no turning being resorted to. After a period of drying, the pattern is cut with a suitable wooden tool, and is coated entirely with coloured clays about as thick as an egg-shell, when a further period of drying has to be undergone. The spaces between the cut lines is then filled with clay-slips which have been coloured by the admixture of various oxides. These are applied rather thick, leaving the pattern in slight relief.

Then comes the finishing, which may be very simple or very elaborate, and consists of further raising with thick clay paste. Further effects may be produced by modelling or by incised lines. Nothing is now required but drying and firing, but this final operation is no easy task. First it is burnt at a low heat, say 850 centigrade, and when cool taken from the kiln and coated with a clear uncoloured plumbic glaze. It is then returned to the kiln and fired to the highest possible heat, say 1050 or 1100 centigrade. Success now depends on many things, and I can only say that I have found that small kilns cannot as a rule be depended upon. If the temperature has not been too high or too low — if the fumes of combustion have not entered the saggers — if no sand has fallen on the glaze — if no bubbling of the glaze has occurred — if the atmosphere has neither been too reducing nor too oxidising — well, then the best quality of "Elton Ware" may be expected.

An enamelling kiln was first used, now a sagger-kiln has taken its place; that is the only difference between now and then; and early specimens of "Elton Ware" may be found which do not compare unfavourably with those of 1910. In fact there are fine colours with effects which we have lost the art of producing, and as an example of the sort of thing, I may say that about eight years ago there was a very uncommon crimson red, which we are now unable to produce with any certainty. I myself have only one perfect specimen of this red.

In 1902, a new departure was made, when I began to introduce gold and platinum in decoration. Gilding was easy enough, but the crux in my mind was how to avoid the vulgarity so easily introduced with gold. To avoid this, a series of experiments with precious metals were embarked upon, but some time elapsed before anything with promise of originality rewarded our efforts. One day I noticed a curious appearance, where some gold overlapped the platinum, which seemed likely to give unique and beautiful results if they could be obtained with certainty. This at first looked easy, and several other effects were also evolved. Four in particular struck me as worth working out on a larger scale, namely, "blue platinum crackle," "gold crackle," "bright platinum crackle," and "fiery platinum," so called because of the frosted gold crackle super-imposed on the "platinum crackle."

But, as if to rebuke presumption, troubles now began which took years to overcome. At first the body was very low-fired, and glazed with a very soft glaze, also very low-fired. This caused the ware not to be watertight; also white specks to appear on the glaze through under-firing. Only two specimens of "blue platinum crackle" survived out of the many pieces made, and the process was discontinued owing to the accurate temperature required involving too much uncertainty. "Gold crackle" shared the same fate owing to the same reason. "Bright platinum crackle" and "fiery platinum" were good from an artistic point of view, but I deemed it essential to produce it with a high-fired watertight body. This, however, started a fresh crop of difficulties; the high heat destroyed the regularity of the crackle. The platinum began to take on a blackish hue, and the "fiery platinum" became inferior and lost its brilliancy, though several new effects were accidently produced, the most curious of them being two or three pieces of "gold crackle," which, when removed from the kiln, resembled *copper,* but gold was deposited on the edge of the crackles. The effect was curious and beautiful, but its reproduction has hitherto been found impossible, though attempted again and again. I have taken expert opinion, but can find no explanation of the mystery. It is only within the last few months that the metallic work has once more been produced with fairly certain results.

Time and labour have been ungrudgingly spent, and the development of "Elton Ware" has been a very interesting experience, but its position in the world of ceramic art, and the question whether its production has been worth all the trouble that has been expended on it must, however, be left to others than myself to decide.

Notes on Linthorpe Ware

From a trade brochure, *circa* 1886.

The revival of taste, marvellous in its extent and eminently pleasing in its results, that has of late years taken place, is a hopeful and encouraging sign that Art, when properly and judiciously applied to articles of everyday use, or of objects that constantly meet the eye, is exercising a happy, wide-spreading and beneficial influence on the minds of the people, and thereby, while promoting their happiness and enjoyment, becoming an important factor in their intellectual progress.

It is the province of the Art-Manufacturer to create where it has not before existed, and to foster wherever its germ can be found, a love for the beautiful; and by his productions to develop that taste-inspiring love until it asserts itself in every surrounding of the "Home" and in every article of utility or ornament. As this influence becomes extended, the application of true artistic principles and feeling to the production of objects of utility will assuredly become more and more a necessity, and the result, so devoutly to be wished, will be that articles devoid of pure form, or that are crude in their style of ornamentation, will be discarded.

This growing revival and development of taste has, as a natural consequence, created an ever-increasing demand for works of more genuinely artistic character than those to which the generation of thirty years ago were accustomed, and in no branch of industry has that demand been so emphatically and lavishly met as in Ceramics. The Potter has felt that on him — the producer of vessels of daily and hourly use in cottage and palace alike — devolves the duty of educating the public taste, and he has with commendable zeal and liberality of outlay set himself to his task and brought to bear upon his productions a wealth and variety of colour, a limitless power and expansion of design, and an ever-increasing manipulative skill that no other branch of manufacture can vie with.

The demand thus alluded to led, a few years back, to the establishment at Linthorpe, near Middlesbrough-on-Tees, of a manufactory devoted to the production of Pottery such as had not previously been successfully attempted in England, or indeed in Europe. The experiment proved eminently satisfactory, and the "Linthorpe Ware" stands out prominent above the productions of other places, as a simple and tasteful proof of the power possessed by Art, when allied to Science, of transmuting the lowliest of all substances into works of the highest intrinsic value. Made of the commonest material — clay — it has had, in the hands of the artist, imparted to it attributes of beauty which have given it a high position as a Ware of great and growing excellence.

Unique in many of its characteristics, it is, by its varied and harmonious, as well as richly blended and flowing, colouring, fitted for every decorative purpose. Its colours, ranging from the quietest blue or green to the most brilliant orange or crimson, with all their intermediate and never-ending varieties and minglings of tone, tint, and depth, are rich in the extreme; and the seekers after soft and quiet, or stronger and more effective, colours, find in it all that their most fastidious tastes can yearn for. The Western idea, until the advent of these Works, has been to look for too much evenness of colour, rather than that variety of tone and depth which adds so much richness and beauty to the Pottery of the East, but this has now all been changed.

The "Linthorpe Ware" is, moreover, strikingly original. For many years the European potter worked on within clear and well-defined lines, beyond which he apparently neither dared or cared to venture. It is indeed doubtful whether, until a comparatively recent date, either the operative or the manufacturer were aware how crude and barbaric were their attempts at decoration. The Eastern potter, on the other hand, endowed with the skill inherited from many generations of artists, long held undisputed supremacy in nearly every branch of this ancient and charming handicraft. Of late, however, this supremacy has been overthrown. The "Linthorpe" productions meet the Oriental potter on his own ground, and boldly challenge careful comparison with the most famous of the ancient or modern glazed Wares of Asia. Whilst reproducing, in all their splendid beauty, many of the finest colour-harmonies of the East, some glorious effects of colouring, never previously produced, are peculiarly its own; and over the whole there is thrown that touch of Occidental thought needed to bring it into harmonious union with our Western ideas and requirements.

These results have not been achieved without labour and without effort. As in all undertakings of an experimental character, the obstacles, difficulties, and disappointments to be contended with have been many and serious. All these in their turn have, however, been nobly encountered and successfully overcome, and the "Ware" now stands pre-eminent over others in its unique beauty, purity, and excellence.

Whilst enormous sums of money are freely given for old specimens of Chelsea, Derby, Bristol, and other famed makes of china, which, as a rule, are valuable mainly because of their age, association, and rarity, here the lover of true beauty may obtain, for a mere trifle, a specimen in which there is not only grace of outline but a combination of colour-harmonies seldom or never met with elsewhere.

The glorious colouring of some of the best specimens of Oriental workmanship command prices which only the wealthy can afford to pay. Here again an opportunity is presented, to people of moderate means, of possessing a vase or other object equal in colour and decorative effect to the best Persian, Chinese, or Japanese productions, but at a vastly less cost. It may not be out of place to quote a recent instance illustrative of this statement. A piece of supposed ancient Oriental pottery, in a famous but lost colour, was offered at half-a-guinea, whilst the same form and colour in "Linthorpe" could be bought for less than one-fifth of that sum. On close examination the piece so offered was found to be actually a "Linthorpe" specimen, which had been sent to the East and returned as a true Oriental production! It would be difficult, indeed, to imagine any evidence more conclusive of success as a rival of the historic productions of the world-famous potters than this.

Whilst richly blended and flowing colours are the main characteristics, and are justly looked upon as the perfection of the Pottery, other and more elaborate forms of ornamentation are successfully attempted. Amongst these is a new and beautiful "Faience," which, in some respects, may be affirmed as even more strikingly original than the "Ware." It is decorated with many pleasing and charming subjects, principally floral. The soft rich colouring so peculiar to the "Ware," and giving it much of its artistic worth, is, in the "Faience," replaced by a brilliant floral decoration on a subdued background of generally two colours, the one gradually fading into and harmonising with the other. The manipulation is most delicate — the gradation of colour being almost imperceptible.

Where lightness and delicacy are desired, perforation becomes an essential adjunct in the working out of the design. Many pleasing effects are thus produced — an airiness and grace being oftentimes imparted to an object that could not be obtained in any other way.

There are also specimens of what is known as "Impasto" work. Here floral ornament is laid upon the object whilst in the "biscuit" stage, in coloured enamels which are toned to contrast pleasantly with the body; the whole being then covered with a coloured glaze, so harmonised with the subject as to enrich and beautify the treatment.

One of the methods pursued is an adaptation of the true Faience, which, first becoming known in Spain during the 15th and 16th centuries, passed thence through the Majorcas and Italy into France. The method originally adopted is at present in total abeyance amongst modern potters. It consisted in laying upon the body of the Ware a coating of Stanniferous enamel; this coating forming the surface upon which the subject chosen by the artist was painted. Some of the most famous and valuable specimens in existence were so produced.

The methods so successfully practised at Urbino and Faienza, and the Barbotine of the earlier French Schools, as distinguished from the modern perversion of the method (and its name,) are brought under contribution and made to render service. Incised, carved, and bas-relief work all play their part.

One of the most recent developments is the production of ornament of a geometrical or strongly conventional character by means of the Linthorpe Glazes, painted in the manner of enamels. This description of ornament being characterised by lightness of colour is peculiarly adapted for the decoration of Salad Bowls and objects for the Luncheon and Tea Table.

It may be said, in conclusion, that nearly all the processes known to the illustrious artists of the Renaissance, so far as they are applicable to the work done at Linthorpe, are there successfully practised.

It is the aim of the art-workers employed to throw expression and feeling into each production, and the various Plaques, Tazzas, Vases, &c., all evince at once the power and beauty of decoration when applied in accordance with the immutable princples of Art.

Although decoration and adornment are such prominent features in Linthorpe Ceramics, the primary idea of all pottery — that of utility — is by no means overlooked. As the late Owen Jones, and the best art-teachers who have followed in his footsteps, have never ceased to inculcate, decoration must ever be subservient to the purpose for which an object is made; and this is a principle never lost sight of in the production of these Works.

Amongst the many hundreds of forms produced it can scarcely be said that any one style predominates, the idea being to procure elegance of outline and beauty of colour wherever suggested. Here we have, it may be, something resembling a prehistoric British shape, whilst there we find a vase suggestive of Japan. Here is an Anglo-Saxon bowl, and there a Peruvian vessel from the tombs; and Indian, Egyptian, Greek, Roman, Moorish, Celtic and Mediaeval examples are to be found on all sides. Many of the articles have, moreover, been designed to meet some particular end or requirement and numbers of them are specially adapted for mounting in silver or other metals.

At the three International Exhibitions where the productions have been shown they have gained distinction. At Calcutta in 1883-4, a Bronze Medal and Certificate were awarded, a similar Medal was given at the World's Industrial and Cotton Centennial Exposition at New Orleans, in 1884-5, and at the Alexandra Palace in 1885, a Gold Medal and Diploma of Merit were awarded by the Jurors.

In conclusion, all who wish to decorate their homes with objects that will not *pall* on the taste nor weary the eye, will do well to make themselves acquainted with the Linthorpe productions. The varied colours of the Ware in their chromatic harmony and the beautiful painting of the Faience, tend to make a room pleasant and delightful. In homes quietly decorated with objects exhibiting culture and refinement "Linthorpe" finds its true place.

Burmantofts Faience

Reports 'from our Leeds Correspondent' which appeared in *The Artist,* II (1881), p. 3 and p. 267.

Nearly one hundred and ten years ago the first pottery was established at Leeds, in Jack-Lane, Hunslet. This, with the old windmill used for grinding flints, is still standing, and is still used for the manufacture of common ware. When the company founded the pottery, Wedgwood's beautiful Queen's ware was in high favour; and to making this cream-coloured ware the company first turned their attention, producing some very beautiful work, and outdistancing by a long way all other imitators of Wedgwood, English and foreign. They did more than imitate Wedgwood, however; they made a kind of ware peculiarly their own, which in turn was imitated by other makers in Staffordshire and elsewhere. The perforated and embossed work is well-known to old china collectors. A great deal was made for exportation to the continent, where many of their finest productions have been discovered and brought back by collectors. A change in taste came; and in 1829 the company failed.

It is not my intention, however, to write a history of the Leeds potteries; but to draw attention to a new faience that is now being manufactured at Leeds, the first attempt at art pottery since the failure of the old Leeds pottery. Many potteries have been established at Leeds since then, but only for ware of the coarsest kind; the art element being totally neglected until quite recently, when it remained for Messrs. Wilcock, of Burmantofts, a firm of firebrick and drain-pipe manufacturers, to produce a faience of real art merit, from clay found on the site of the pottery, rather less than a mile from the centre of the town. This material is mined for and found in a rocky state. No less than four different kinds of clay are found at various depths, as well as the coal used in burning it.

The ware is characterised by its hardness, thick majolica-like glaze, and warmth of colour, giving valuable effect in a room. It may be divided into two heads, that for architectural and that for domestic ornament. The architectural faience is made in large and small pieces, or rather blocks, and is used for interior as well as exterior decoration; the advantage over tiles being that it may be built into the structure, and not merely laid on the surface, where from its imperfect adherence it may be liable to come off, especially in either hot or damp places, although wall tiles are made in it for use in halls and on fireplaces, &c. Out of the architectural faience sprang the manufacture of vases, &c., it having been suggested that the same ware and style of work might be applied for decorative purposes; and although working in a rather different groove, this branch bids fair to become a formidable rival to Messrs. Doulton's Lambeth ware.

The body is a mixture which is the invention of Messrs. Wilcock, and is based on the finest kind of fireclay. This is baked at a most intense heat, and is covered with a rich thick glaze, coloured in various tones of warm olive greens, citrons, browns, and sometimes a fine dark blue. This glaze, owing to the great heat employed, is thoroughly incorporated or fused into the body. In certain instances raised ornaments or sunk patterns are covered by a glaze of a different colour to the rest of the piece, and give very good effects, by a judicious choice of harmonious colours. A pair of vases treated in this manner I greatly admired; gourd-shaped, with marigolds in relief; the body of the vase was coloured a citrine green, and the flowers a very curious pale neutral blue, harmonising very beautifully with the ground of the vase. The general ornamentation of the ware is either incised or in relief, and frequently on some of the vases in combination. Where it is practicable all this is done by hand when the clay is in a soft state, and each piece or set may be said to be unique, there being seldom replicas made.

The principal decoration is generally derived from the floral world, conventionalized; and, on some larger plaques, classical subjects are introduced. The much abused Japanese style is sparingly used, and where it is, it is far from being in the silly incongruous manner instanced in the *Artist* of last month. The wall tiles are generally ornamented in high relief with vigourously designed patterns; these, of course, are cast from a mould or pressed. They are made too with patterns incised by hand. Among the flat ware made are large slabs for building up into mantelpieces, as well as some very large panels, nearly five feet high, for exterior decoration having well-modelled floral designs.

Most of the work is designed and, of course, all executed, at the pottery by a staff of English workmen and artists, though in some few instances they are indebted to foreign artists for the designs, chiefly, I believe, for the classical subjects.

The work is on the whole of a most high order of merit, and though at present little known, owing to it being very little exhibited, it will soon, I think, be well appreciated if it be carried on in the same spirit as it is being at present. It is in a healthy and truly artistic taste, with which all lovers of good ceramic art will be well pleased.

We are very proud of our new art pottery in Leeds here: since I sent you an account of it last January (see "A Keramic Revival" in that month's number) it has made rapid and progressive strides. The ware, too, has almost changed its character, and I think attained more originality.

A great many experiments have been going on with regard to body, colours, and firing; and considering the recent establishment of the pottery (that is the fine art portion of it) with a marked success. Upon the degree of heat employed depends of course the perfection or the reverse of the colour, a trifle more or less being a great consideration. but as a result of these trials the regulation of heat is now well understood and under command, and consequently the effect certain.

In looking round the workrooms crowded with ware one is struck by the infinite variety combined with individuality. As I said before, each piece is unique, and, what might cause a pang in the heart of some whose perception of "balance" is strongly developed, there are no *pairs!* Vases of a similar size and shape there are, but it would be rather hard to find any two which would suit the taste of such a person, with respect to duplicate decoration.

The body of the ware has undergone a change, too. It is now made of a fine red clay, which, if baked without glaze, would produce a very fine red and close terra cotta. On this base the artist with his range of colours has great scope for effect; for by using opaque colours he can entirely cover the ground, or by the same colours used rather thinner, and in places leaving the ground, the rich red of the body comes well into the general decoration.

New colours and combinations too have been found; no trifling matter this, considering the limited range of colours capable of standing the heat required to fuse the glaze; for all decoration is here under the glaze, and till these last few years various blues from oxide of cobalt formed the only underglaze colour known to potters, which was not precluded by its price from extensive use. What seems a rather new idea, and is found to answer well, is the using of the colours on the ware while it is yet in a soft state. It is then dipped in the glaze, and in some of the experiments baked in a "green" state with good results.

It is a rather difficult task to describe the appearance of the ware. Such of your London readers as are interested will find specimens, I believe, at Howell & James's; but in the meanwhile I will do my best to give a slight idea of a few pieces.

One of the best batches turned out is a series of bottles and jars in the African style; gourd shaped bottles, and some quaint looking nests of small jars fastened together. Then there are some pilgrim shaped bottles, for hanging up. All these are richly coloured and glazed with apple and yellow greens, with patterns incised, sometimes through the glaze, showing the red body underneath. In a higher style of art are some well proportioned vases decorated with a blending of colours; greys, brown, purples, here and there streaked with yellow, and the whole forming an exquisite agate-like effect, reminding you forcibly of some of the fine agate ware made by Wedgwood and Bentley.

Other pieces are covered with well modelled flowers in high relief, blended backgrounds, the flowers naturally coloured. The principal artist, M. Kreimer, is very successful in this as well as in modelling large plaques with figure subjects.

I may add that all this, by the feeling and energy of Mr. Holroyd, the manager, has emanated from the manufacture of drain pipes, and it is no little to this gentleman's credit that such a high class of pottery is produced from materials found on the spot, the clay being literally got from a mine under the pottery itself.

Leeds: 16 August, 1881.

Modern Decorative Wares

An article by Wilton P. Rix describing *flambé* glazed pottery and other more commercial wares of the Edwardian era; it appeared in the *Art Journal*, 1905, p. 113.

The unlimited resources of pottery as a decorative medium never fail to fascinate the craftsman. Unlike that of the jeweller, the material itself has no intrinsic worth. Its artistic merit alone can enhance its value. To the ordinary observer it may seem that little remains to be achieved in the potter's art. It may indeed be true that the fundamental processes have already been brought near to perfection; yet the possible changes and combinations of form, texture, colour, glaze, and body are still practically unlimited. Hence the designer of today, to whom the discovery of new treatments still affords such varied opportunity, is often tempted to encumber his material with meretricious enrichments, mistaking skilful technique for artistic merit.

The most original and decorative types of pottery in the past have been marked by a freedom from this undue elaboration. Simplicity and directness of aim have indeed constituted the greatest charm of ceramic art. Though there are notable exceptions, it is impossible to suppress the conviction that the enterprise lately shown in the production of artistic pottery of high merit is by no means equal to that displayed in the working of metal, glass, jewellery, and paperhanging. Pottery and porcelain, though offering far greater opportunity, have been during the last few years singularly barren in this respect.

One possible cause of this decadence is that its true position as a decorative accessory has been left too much to chance. The utmost care and thought are lavished on the architectural details of the home - the metal fittings, hangings, and wall treatments; but the pottery, which should give an accent of colour harmonising with the design and general effect of the surroundings, is often left haphazard to the untutored selection of some wholesale furnisher. The overwhelming supply and low price of inartistic bric-a-brac has also tended to degrade the popular appreciation of decorative pottery as a whole: and against this the maker of works of enduring merit, even with the best intentions, finds it difficult to contend.

In fact, the characteristics of modern pottery have become too ephemeral. Until it is again regarded as an object worthy to enshrine enduring and aesthetic ideals, pottery must fail to regain its legitimate place as an article of *vertu*.

Ceramic decoration in England, as in France, has of late years emancipated itself considerably from the meretricious and realistic. The result has been steady progress in the public acceptance of a more robust treatment, which, however, occasionally inclines towards appreciation of methods altogether too bizarre.

Among the developments of the last two or three years, it is interesting to notice that the most striking have been chiefly influenced by new advances in technical skill. Thus the careful study of the behaviour of crystalline glazes, the efficient control of matt textures, and other similar results involving the accurate treatment of vaporous atmosphere in the kiln, have all played an important part in securing new decorative effects.

Indeed, it may be said that texture and colour have lately received quite a large share of consideration as elements in the modern designer's scheme, elaboration of detail and delicacy of finish being mostly relegated to a secondary position. All these methods are largely dependent for their success on scientific control of the firing process, which has generally been left too much in unskilled hands.

Among other examples, the very admirable productions of ruby lustre on both matt and full-glazed surfaces, which have lately rewarded the efforts of Mr. Owen Carter, deserve mention. The amazing variety of iridescence to be obtained by the vaporous method of kiln-firing always adds a charm to this type of ware.

Extreme care is demanded in deciding the most opportune moment for the evolution of wood smoke in the muffle which can alone produce the desired effects, and this must always tax the best skill of the potter. There are good examples, which may be said in many respects to deserve a place among the well-known works of Maw, De Morgan, and Lachenal.

No doubt the interest attaching to such production is largely dependent on accidental effects which have hitherto baffled the control of the potter, and it is due to the persistence of a few enterprising spirits that some advance has been made.

As an example of such mastery of the elusive in ceramics the "Rouge Flambé" of the Doulton pottery is worthy of the highest praise. Though some have regarded the beautiful "sang-de-boeuf" glazes as mere revivals of the lost art of the Chinese, there is added to the rediscovery that element of control which is the best guarantee of further progress.

To Mr. Bernard Moore undoubtedly belongs the credit of the first reproduction of these old effects. Beyond this, he is also to be congratulated on the inspiration he has given to Mr. Cuthbert Bailey, whose persevering study of technical conditions has enabled him to bring from the kiln many pieces of "Rouge Flambé," "Peach Blow," and "Haricot" which vie with the best examples of the East. The rich effects of copper glazes fused in a reducing fire have been realised and guarded jealously by the Chinese for centuries, but they have long ceased to produce the best types of the "sang-de-boeuf" and ruby glazes which are the pride of our greatest art collections. These modern productions, however, are the more striking because they have attained also the richly blended yellow, blue, green and purple tints which so enhanced the value of the ancient pieces. From the nature of the process of vaporous firing, each piece is obviously liable to some variation; an individuality is thus secured in each specimen which commends the ware to the collector and better justifies its claim to a place among the triumphs of the potter.

It is curious to note that in another field of ceramics equally elusive, namely, that of crystalline glazes, the potter of today has been venturing successfully. As in vaporous fired glazes and lustres, so in crystalline textures: the desired effects are largely dependent on the accurate control of the uncertainties of firing and cooling.

As often happens, two well-known potteries have simultaneously pursued this line of research, while adopting widely different treatments.

The Sabrina ware of the Worcester Royal Porcelain Works is certainly unique in character and method. By saturation of the porcelain body with certain metallic solutions under accurate conditions of firing, the growth of starry crystals is induced during the cooling of the ware. The variety of decorative interest thus realised is considerable, and evidently capable of further extension.

Somewhat akin to this in its object, yet differing in method, is the Lancastrian ware lately introduced by Mr. William Burton, whose skill as a practical ceramist has long been established. The Continental potters have already pursued the same attempt with varying success, notably at Copenhagen, Sèvres, Rorstrand and Berlin. In the Lancastrian ware, however, advantage has been taken of opalescence as an added factor in the treatment, and to layers, streaks, and feathery gradations of colour are added groups of crystalline forms entangled and embedded in the glaze itself. The examples of this ware displayed in London last year, at the Society of Arts and elsewhere, show what decorative resources are still available to the potter, when artistic judgment and technical skill are combined in its production.

Wholly different in character, yet remarkable for its robust and simple decoration, is the Celtic garden terra-cotta made by Messrs. Liberty. The designs are, many of them, by Mrs. G.F. Watts, whose discriminating direction of the modellers at the Compton Pottery has held a large share in this revival of Celtic art. In its present application it harmonises more readily with the landscape garden than the forms to which one has been accustomed in the Italian *parterre*.

In another form the increasing desire for glazed exterior construction and enrichments has been notably met by Mr. Harold Rathbone, who has persistently devoted himself to the production of enamelled ware of the Della Robbia type, with no small amount of success.

Much discriminating perception in form and colour is apparent in the best examples, while the exigencies of the material are carefully studied; considerable versatility of treatment is also shown, without any undue forcing of the method beyond its obvious limitations. The productions of several other decorative potters deserve notice. Among these may be named the very skilful treatment of *fungoid* growths in raised outline by Mr. Moorcroft; and also the examples of 'Sgraffito' in coloured parian bodies, by Mr. F.W. Rhead, of the Foley Potteries. It is only possible to call attention to them as additional instances of healthy advance in appreciation of the increasing resources available to the ceramic designer.

Developments in Martinware

An anonymous article entitled 'Some recent developments in the pottery ware of the Martin Brothers', which appeared in *The Studio* XL11 (1908), pp. 109 - 115.

We have on several occasions drawn the attention of readers of THE STUDIO to certain features in the pottery of Japan which are usually ignored by students of ceramic art, although, as a matter of fact, they display evidences of the most skilled craftsmanship. The idea that art is only exhibited in pottery when it is covered with painted ornament is still very firmly impressed in the minds of many people, who would deny all aesthetic qualities of the potter's craft which do not show the painter's craftsmanship and skill. In saying this, it must not be thought that we underrate the painter's beautiful art when applied to the decoration of porcelain or earthenware; our preferences are, however, for those features which are essentially characteristic of the potter's craft - the manipulation of clays of varied texture and of coloured glazes, and of such decorative treatment as essentially belongs to the potter's art, and bears no resemblance to that of other crafts. The work of the old Japanese potters is particularly rich in these qualities. Kenzan, Ninsei, Rokubei, and many others produced wares which were full of individuality, and displayed the intimate and extensive knowledge which they possessed of their craft, and an aesthetic perception which is too often lacking in modern European and American productions.

Indeed it is rarely that the separate achievements of any Western potter contain evidence of such comprehension and skill as may be found in those of the Far East. Yet, it may gratefully be admitted that there have been a few workers in France, Germany, and England, who, in recent years, have taken some delight in developing the true qualities of their craft, and have given to each object which has come from their hands a distinction not to be found in the general mass of contemporary ceramic work. Among the honoured names of such craftsmen those of the Martin Brothers, of London, are especially worthy of distinction. For many years past these artists have produced from year to year a few objects, which have been for the most part eagerly sought for by collectors and others. Much of their early work depended for its main interest on the incised decoration of birds, fish or flowers with which it was enriched. But during the last few years they have materially broadened their point of view, and have sought after and obtained many original modes of expression which lend to their productions a charm which, without being in any way imitative, recalls the work of the old potters of Japan. We shall purposely confine our remarks to these later features of their work, as we consider them to be of especial interest at this time.

The few examples we now illustrate may be examined with advantage from two points of view - one in relation to the technical qualities of their production, the other to the characteristics of their ornament. Of their technical qualities it may be remarked that the earths employed, while varied in character, are uniformly dense in consistency and of excellent quality. The decoration is usually obtained by the use of "slip", either incised in the *Mishima* style of Japan, or applied to the surface with a brush. Salt glaze in connection with coloured enamels is judiciously employed, and the makers have been especially successful in the production of a very fine dullish black, which has all the excellent qualities of the best Chinese prototypes. The quaint and irregular shapes given to the various objects are uncommon without being bizarre. The decoration is, for the most part, intimately connected with the manufacture of the object, and not, as it were, an afterthought. In this respect their later work differs materially from some of their earlier, and is proportionately the more commendable.

When Nature decorates her own productions, such as an egg, a shell, a flower or a fruit, she does not reproduce the forms of other natural objects. She does not paint a lily on an egg, a bird on a shell, a fish on a flower, or the portrait of a man on a fruit. Each one of these objects has a simple type of decoration of probably more or less use to its existence, or it may be the outcome of form and growth.

It would seem to us that the Martin Brothers, consciously or unconsciously, have endeavoured to follow these precepts of Nature, and in doing so have borrowed many ideas from eggs and shells and other natural forms, not in strict imitation, but as suggestions for suitable ornament. For example, the "slip" decoration on figure 1, without being a copy of the markings upon a melon, seems to us to have been suggested by them; that of figure 2 - an excellent one to bring out the "broken" colour of running glazes - might have resulted from the appearance of a corn-cob, from which the grain has been extracted. Figures 3, 4, 5 and 6 have characteristics of surface, form or decoration, which remind one of certain sea-shells or sea-weed; Figure 7 displays the net-like structure of certain organisms; Figure 8 has a texture not unlike that of a cabbage; Figure 9, the skin of a wild animal; while figure 10 simulates in its colour and texture an egg. To have imitated exactly such objects would have been inappropriate and inartistic; but to have allowed them to suggest a scheme of ornamentation adapted to the technical requirements and qualities of the material is entirely permissible.

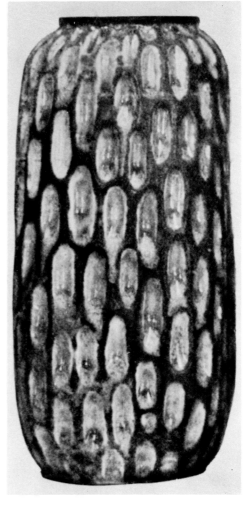

Figure 1 *Figure 2*

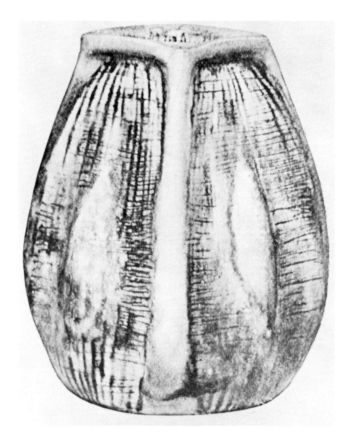

Figure 3

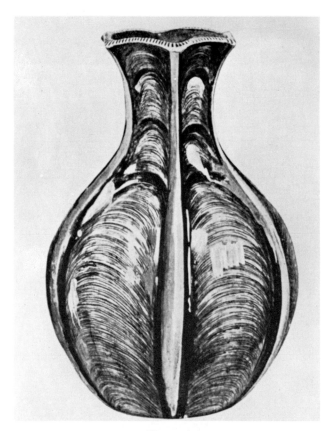

Figure 4

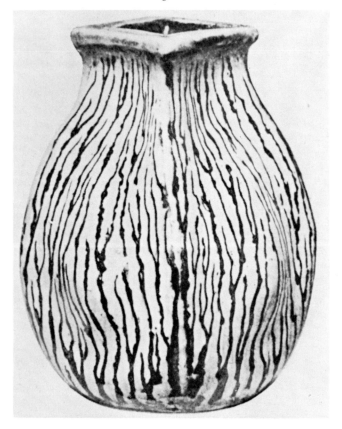

Figure 5

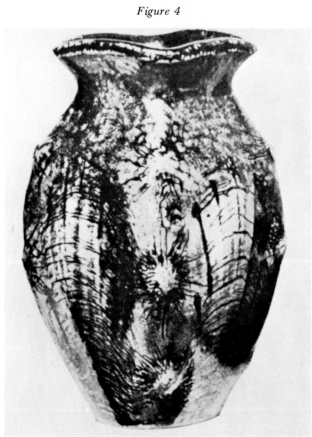

Figure 6

The striations on figure 1 follow and accentuate the form of the vase, breaking up the surface into pleasant irregularity, and display the coloured enamel to great advantage. Figure 2 is simply another device apparently selected with the same object in view. Figures 3 and 4, with their shell-like qualities of surface, are admirable examples of the clever manipulation of glazes - figure 4 being, indeed, a *chef d'oeuvre* of the potter's art - alike perfect in potting and glazing. The striations in the panels are incised and not painted.

Incised pattern filled in with paste of a different colour to the body of the ware, which we have referred to as *Mishima,* was a favourite method of decoration of the old Corean and Japanese potters. It is a class of ornamentation which can only be produced by the potter himself, as it must be completed while the clay is in a damp state, before it is fired. It is one which has been somewhat neglected in Europe. In recent years the Dutch potters have practised it to a limited extent, but no work has been produced in the West of this character to compare in excellence with that of the Yatsushiro potters. Figures 11 to 16 are types of this class made by the Martin Brothers, and they have the merit of being quite original in conception. The other examples here illustrated are selected to show a few more of the many varieties of form and treatment, and help to display the makers' power of invention and diversity of treatment.

Figure 7

Figure 8

Figure 9

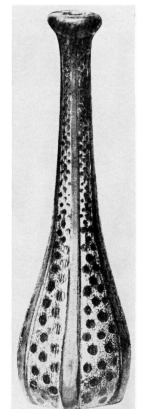

Figure 11

Figure 10

Figure 12

Figure 13

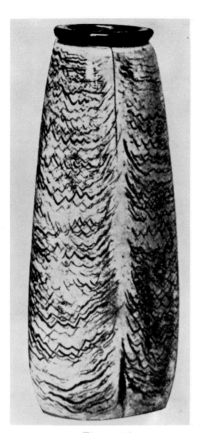

Figure 14

Figure 15

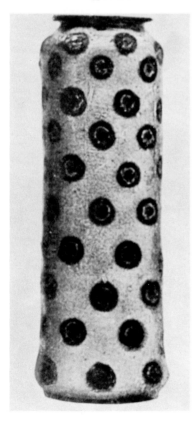

Figure 16

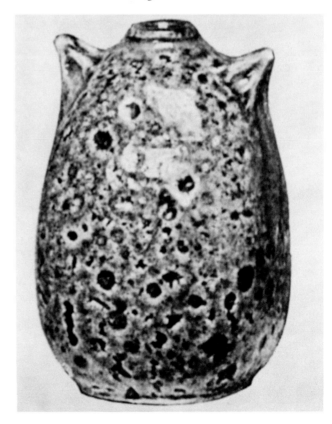

Figure 17

One is apt, without careful examination, to fail to give full credit to the potter for the laborious and skilful manipulation necessary to the successful production of *Mishima* decoration. The Martin Brothers have been singularly happy in their efforts in this direction, and their departure in style from all previous examples is most commendable. This inlaid work is open to numerous variations and developments, and there will be no necessity for them in future years to repeat their earlier successes. And of this there need be no fear, if they continue to work upon the admirable lines they have hitherto followed.

The Martins have an excellent plan of incising in the foot or back of each piece their name and the date of its production. One may thus trace the special successes of each year, and all spurious imitations may be readily detected. By the avoidance of imitation and repetition, and by the faculty of invention and knowledge of the possibilities of his craft, there is no reason why the potter should not in the future, as he has done upon rare occasions in the past, rise to the greatest distinction as an artist, and we cannot but feel that the Martin Brothers are on the right road to such an eminence.

Our thanks are due to the Artificers' Guild, Maddox Street, London, for their permission to illustrate the examples reproduced in figures 1, 2, 16, 24 and 26 from their varied collection.

Figure 18

Figure 20

Figure 19

Figure 21

Figure 22

Figure 23

Figure 24

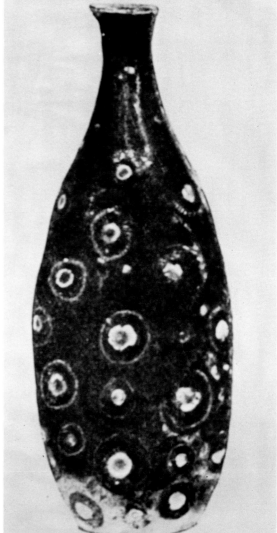

Figure 25   *Figure 26*

Figure 1. Pair of vases, stoneware. Doulton and Co., decorated by Hannah B. Barlow. Dated 1874.

Figure 2. Plaque, stoneware. Doulton and Co., modelled by George Tinworth. Height 6½ins. Circa 1880.

Figure 3. Bowl, stoneware. Doulton and Co. (?), modelled by Mark V. Marshall (the piece bears no factory mark). Height 8½ins. Circa 1880.

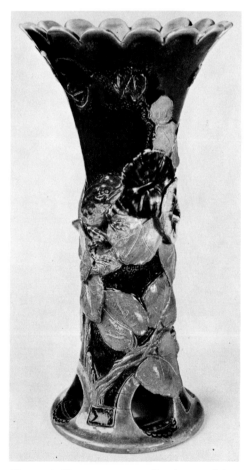

Figure 4. Vase, stoneware, Doulton and Co., modelled by Mark V. Marshall (the piece bears no factory mark, but is incised with a Doulton assistant's mark). Height 10¼ins. Circa 1880.

Figure 5. Vase, stoneware. Doulton and Co., decorated by Louisa E. Edwards. Height 10ins. Dated 1877.

Figure 6. Vase, stoneware. Doulton and Co., decorated by Edith D. Lupton. Height 14ins. Dated 1882.

Figure 7. Vase, stoneware. Doulton and Co., decorated by Francis E. Lee. Height 22ins. Dated 1884.

Figure 8. Vase, stoneware. Doulton and Co. Height 10ins. Dated 1886.

Figure 9. Vase, stoneware. Doulton and Co., decorated by Mark V. Marshall (the piece bears no factory mark, but is painted with the initials of Doulton assistants). Height 9ins. Dated 1889.

Figure 10. Vase, stoneware. Doulton and Co., decorated by Florence E. Barlow. Height 13ins. Circa 1895.

Figure 11. Vase, stoneware. Doulton and Co., decorated by Eliza Simmance. Height 9¼ins. Circa 1895.

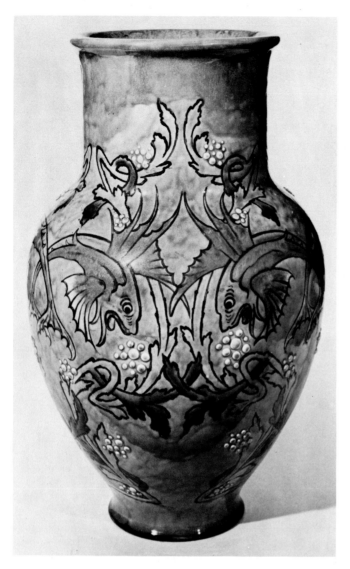

Figure 12. Vase, stoneware. Doulton and Co., decorated by Eliza Simmance. Height 14¼ins. Circa 1900.

Figure 13. Vase, stoneware. Doulton and Co., modelled by Frank C. Pope. Height 12¾ins. Circa 1910.

Figure 14. Vase, stoneware. Doulton Silicon (Doulton and Co.), decorated by Eliza Simmance. Height 4¼ins. dated 1884.

Figure 15. Pair of flasks, stoneware. Doulton Silicon (Doulton and Co.), decorated by Eliza Simmance. Height 10¼ins. Circa 1885.

Figure 16. Bowl on stand, stoneware. Doulton Silicon (Doulton and Co.). Height 4¾ins. Dated 1885.

Figure 17. Vase, stoneware. C.J.C. Bailey, made by Edgar Kettle. Height 10ins. Dated 1874.

Figure 18. Vase, stoneware. C.J.C. Bailey, made by Edgar Kettle. Height 10½ins. Dated 1875.

Figure 19. Vase, stoneware. C.J.C. Bailey, decorated by E. Bennett. Height 12ins. Dated 1888.

Figure 20. Bowl, stoneware. C.J.C. Bailey. Height 3¾ins. Circa 1880.

*Figure 21. Tobacco-jar, stoneware. C.J.C. Bailey. Height 5¼ins.
Circa 1880.*

*Figure 22. Vase, stoneware. Martin Brothers. Height
19ins. Dated 1875.*

*Figure 23. Jug, stoneware. Martin Brothers.
Height 11½ins. Dated 1894.*

*Figure 24. Pair of vases, stoneware. Martin Brothers. Height
13¼ins. Dated 1897.*

Figure 25. Vase, stoneware. Martin Brothers. Height 8ins. Dated 1892.

Figure 26. Tobacco-jar, stoneware. Martin Brothers. Height (including base) 16¼ins. Circa 1895.

Figure 27. Jug, stoneware. Martin Brothers. Height 5½ins. Dated 1880.

Figure 28. Plaque, earthenware. Minton's Art-Pottery Studio, painted by W.S. Coleman. Diameter 13½ins. Dated 1870.

Figure 29. Plaque, earthenware. Minton's Art-Pottery Studio. Diameter 13½ins. Dated 1870.

Figure 30. Plaque, earthenware. Minton's Art-Pottery Studio. Diameter 13¼ins. Dated 1872.

Figure 31. Tile panel, earthenware. Minton's Art-Pottery Studio. Height 16ins. Circa 1872.

Figure 32(a) Spring.

Four tile panels, earthenware. Doulton Faience (Doulton and Co.), painted by John H. McLennan. Height 12ins. Circa 1885.

Figure 32(b) Summer.

Figure 32(c) Autumn.

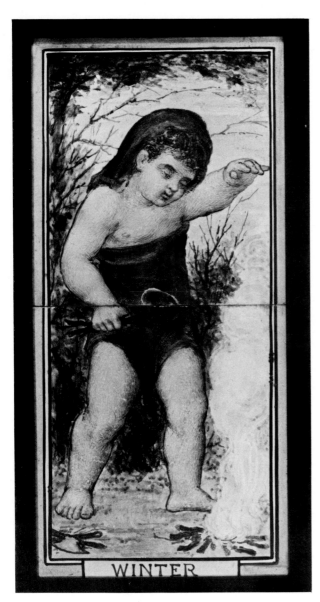

Figure 32(d) Winter.

Figure 33. Vase, earthenware. Doulton Faience (Doulton and Co.), painted by Mary Butterton. Height 8¾ins. Dated 1880.

Figure 34. Jar and cover, earthenware. Doulton Faience (Doulton and Co.), painted by Helen A. Arding. Height 3¼ins. Dated 1880.

Figure 35. Plaque, earthenware. Doulton and Co., painted by Linnie Watt. Diameter 8¼ins. Circa 1880.

Figure 36. Plaque, earthenware. Doulton Faience (Doulton and Co.), painted by Mary Capes. Diameter 13¾ins. Circa 1882 (the piece bears the mark of Pinder, Bourne and Co. which Doulton's bought in 1878, but the title was retained until 1882).

Figure 37. Vase, earthenware. Doulton Impasto (Doulton and Co.), decorated by F.M. Collins. Height 12½ins. Dated 1879.

Figure 38. Vase, earthenware. Doulton Impasto (Doulton and Co.), decorated by Rona Keen. Height 7½ins. Dated 1887.

Figure 39. Plaque, earthenware. Painted by G.B. Willson for Howell & James' Annual Art-Pottery Exhibition. Diameter 16¾ins. Dated 1882.

Figure 40. Plaque, earthenware. Painted for Howell & James'
Annual Art-Pottery Exhibition. Diameter 12ins. Dated 1881.

Figure 41. Plaque, earthenware. Painted by J. Edith Cowper
for Howell & James' exhibit at the Paris Exhibition, 1878.
Diameter 10¼ins. Dated 1878.

Figure 42. Plaque, earthenware. Painted by J. Edith Cowper
for Howell & James' exhibit at the Paris Exhibition, 1878.
Diameter 10¼ins. Dated 1878.

Figure 43. Plaque, earthenware. J. Wedgwood and Sons.
Diameter 10¼ins. Dated 1880.

Figure 44. Vase, earthenware. J. Wedgwood and Sons. Height 9½ins. Circa 1880.

Figure 45. Vase, earthenware. Linthorpe Pottery, designed by Christopher Dresser, decorated by William Davison. Height 15ins. Circa 1880.

Figure 47. Dish, earthenware. William De Morgan, decorated by Charles Passenger. Diameter 13¼ins. 1877-1911.

Figure 46. Vase, earthenware. Watcombe Pottery Co. Height 13ins. Circa 1880.

Figure 48. Dish, earthenware. William De Morgan, decorated by Halsey Ricardo. Diameter 14¼ins. 1888-98.

Figure 49. Dish, earthenware. William De Morgan, decorated by Charles Passenger. Diameter 14½ins. 1877-1911.

Figure 50. Vase, earthenware. William De Morgan. Height 6ins. 1888-1897.

Figure 51. Vase, earthenware. William De Morgan. Height 11¾ins. 1888-1911.

Figure 52. Vase, earthenware. William De Morgan. Height 7¼ins. 1882-8.

Figure 53. Vase, earthenware. William De Morgan, decorated by Fred Passenger. Height 15½ins. 1888-97.

Figure 54. Vase, earthenware. William De Morgan, decorated by Fred Passenger. Height 15½ins. 1888-97.

Figure 56. Jug, earthenware. William De Morgan. Height 9¼ins. 1888-97.

Figure 55. Vase, earthenware. William De Morgan, decorated by Fred Passenger. Height 15¼ins. 1888-97.

Figure 57. Vase, earthenware. William De Morgan. Height 10½ins. 1888-97.

Figure 58. Vase, earthenware. William De Morgan. Height 15¾ins. 1882-88.

Figure 59. Vase, earthenware. William De Morgan, decorated by James Hersey. Height 8¼ins. Circa 1890.

Figure 60. Vase, earthenware. William De Morgan. Height 14¾ins. 1888-97.

Figure 62. Vase, earthenware. Maw and Co., designed by Walter Crane. Height 8¾ins. Circa 1890.

Figure 61. Vase, earthenware. Maw and Co., designed by Walter Crane. Height 12¾ins. Dated 1891.

Figure 63. Vase, earthenware. Maw and Co. Height 8¼ins. Dated 1887.

Figure 65. Plaque, earthenware. Craven Dunnill and Co. Diameter 15¼ins. Circa 1890.

Figure 64. Vase, earthenware. Maw and Co. Height 9ins. Circa 1890.

Figure 66. Vase, earthenware. Craven Dunnill and Co. Height 7ins. Circa 1890.

Figure 67. Bowl, earthenware. John Pearson. Diameter 7¾ins. Circa 1890.

Figure 68. Vase, earthenware. Della Robbia Pottery, decorated by Charles Collis and James Fogo. Height 15¼ins. 1894-1906.

Figure 69. Plaque, earthenware. Della Robbia Pottery, modelled by Conrad Dressler. Diameter 3½ins. Dated 1894.

Figure 71. Bowl, earthenware. Della Robbia Pottery, decorated by Annie Smith. Diameter 9½ins. 1894-1906.

Figure 70. Vase, earthenware. Della Robbia Pottery, decorated by James Fogo. Height 11½ins. 1894-1906.

Figure 72. Bowl, earthenware. Della Robbia Pottery. Diameter 7¾ins. 1894-1906.

Figure 73. Vase, earthenware. Della Robbia Pottery. Height 5ins. 1894-1906.

Figure 74. Dish, earthenware. Della Robbia Pottery. Diameter 15¼ins. 1894-1906.

Figure 75. Plaque, earthenware. Della Robbia Pottery, designed by Harold Rathbone after Ford Madox Brown. Height 26ins. Dated 1900.

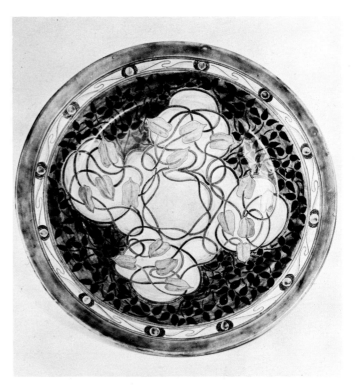

Figure 77. Dish, earthenware. Della Robbia Pottery. Diameter 15ins. Dated 1905.

Figure 76. Vase, earthenware. Della Robbia Pottery, decorated by A.E. Bells. Height 10ins. 1894-1906.

Figure 78. Frieze, earthenware. Della Robbia Pottery, designed by E.M. Rope. Length 46ins. Dated 1895.

Figure 80. Bowl, earthenware. Della Robbia Pottery Co., decorated by Charles Collis and James Hughes. Diameter 7¼ins. 1894-1906.

Figure 79. Vase, earthenware. Della Robbia Pottery Co., decorated by A.E. Bells and Liza Wilkins. Height 12ins. Dated 1898.

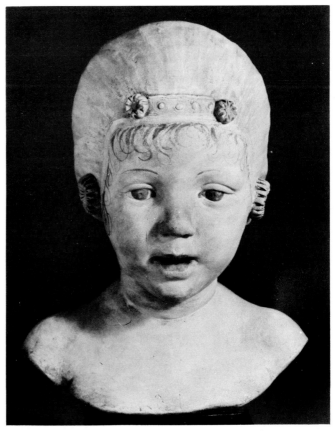

Figure 81. Bust of a young girl, stoneware. Made by Conrad Dressler at the Medmenham Pottery, Marlow, Buckinghamshire. Height (including wooden plinth) 14¾ins. Dated 1895.

Figure 82. Bowl, earthenware. Watcombe Pottery Co. Diameter 7¾ins. Circa 1880.

Figure 83. Vase, earthenware. Watcombe Pottery Co. Height 6ins. Circa 1880.

Figure 84. Vase, earthenware. Watcombe Pottery Co. Height 8ins. Circa 1880.

Figure 85. Vase, earthenware. Watcombe Pottery Co. Height 7¾ins. Circa 1885.

Figure 86. Vase, earthenware. Watcombe Pottery Co. Height 4ins. Circa 1885.

Figure 88. Beaker, earthenware. Torquay Terra-Cotta Co. Height 4¼ins. Circa 1880.

Figure 87. Jar and cover, earthenware. Watcombe Pottery Co. Height 4¾ins. Circa 1885.

Figure 89. Vase, earthenware. Aller Vale Art Potteries. Height 8ins. 1891-1901.

Figure 90. Vase, earthenware. C.H. Brannam. Height 12ins. Dated 1881.

Figure 91. Vase, earthenware. C.H. Brannam, decorated by James Dewdney. Height 10½ins. Dated 1882.

Figure 92. Beaker, earthenware. C.H. Brannam. Height 5½ins. Dated 1883.

Figure 94. Vase, earthenware. C.H. Brannam, decorated by James Dewdney. Height 4¾ins. Dated 1885.

Figure 93. Vase, earthenware. C.H. Brannan. Height 12¾ins. Dated 1885.

Figure 96. Ship-vase, earthenware. C.H. Brannam. Length 12½ins. Dated 1900.

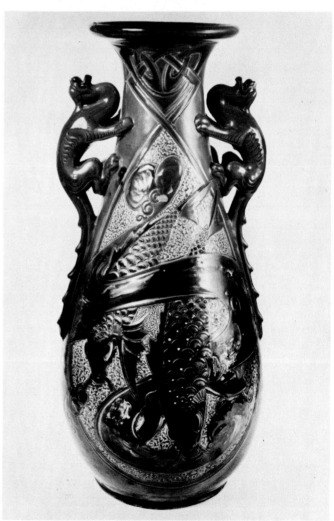

Figure 95. Vase, earthenware. C.H. Brannam, decorated by James Dewdney. Height 19¾ins. Dated 1889.

Figure 97. Vase, earthenware. C.H. Brannam, decorated by James Dewdney. Height 16½ins. Dated 1905.

Figure 98. Charger, earthenware. C.H. Brannam, decorated by R. Cowie. Diameter 15¼ins. Dated 1907.

Figure 99. Vase, earthenware. Alexander Lauder. Height 15½ins. Circa 1880.

Figure 100. Vase, earthenware. Alexander Lauder. Height 7¾ins. Dated 1891.

Figure 101. Vase, earthenware. Edmund Elton. Height 8¾ins. Dated 1882.

Figure 102. Vase, earthenware. Edmund Elton. Height 7½ins. Circa 1890.

Figure 103. Vase, earthenware. Edmund Elton. Height 10ins. Circa 1890.

Figure 104. Jug, earthenware. Linthorpe Pottery, designed by Christopher Dresser. Height 6½ins. Circa 1880.

Figure 105. Vase, earthenware. Linthorpe Pottery, designed by Christopher Dresser. Height 8ins. Circa 1880.

Figure 106. Vase, earthenware. Linthorpe Pottery, designed by Christopher Dresser. Height 6½ins. Circa 1880.

Figure 108. Vase, earthenware. Linthorpe Pottery, designed by Christopher Dresser. Height 5½ins. Circa 1880.

Figure 107. Vase, earthenware. Linthorpe Pottery, designed by Christopher Dresser. Height 10¾ins. Circa 1880.

Figure 109. Vase, earthenware. Linthorpe Pottery, designed by Christopher Dresser. Height 4ins. Circa 1880.

Figure 110. Vase, earthenware. Burmantofts Faience (J. Wilcock). Height 5ins. Circa 1885.

Figure 111. Vase, earthenware. Burmantofts Faience (J. Wilcock). Height 9½ins. Circa 1890.

Figure 113. Vase, earthenware. Burmantofts Faience (J. Wilcock). Height 12ins. Circa 1895.

Figure 112. Vase, earthenware. Burmantofts Faience (J. Wilcock). Height 5½ins. Circa 1885.

Figure 114. Figure of a monkey, earthenware. Burmantofts Faience (J. Wilcock), after a model by V. Kremer (attributed). Height 5¾ins. Circa 1885.

Figure 115. Vase, earthenware. Burmantofts Faience (J. Wilcock), after a model by V. Kremer (attributed). Height 24¾ins. Circa 1885.

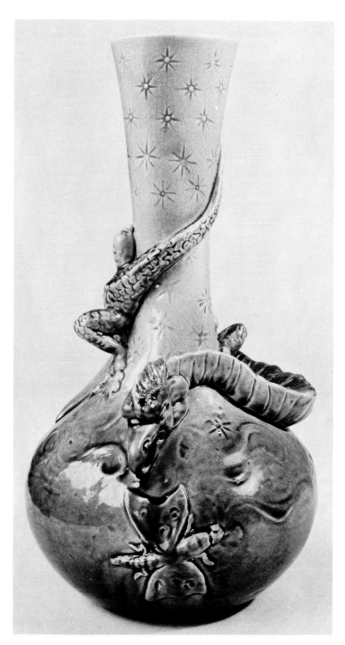

Figure 116. Vase, earthenware. Burmantofts Faience (J. Wilcock), after a model by V. Kremer (attributed). Height 24¼ins. Circa 1885.

Figure 117. Vase, earthenware. Burmantofts Faience (J. Wilcock), after a model by V. Kremer (attributed). Height 11ins. Circa 1885.

Figure 118. Plaque, earthenware. Burmantofts Faience (J. Wilcock). Diameter 20ins. Circa 1885.

Figure 119. Vase, earthenware. Burmantofts Faience (J. Wilcock). Height 14ins. Circa 1885.

Figure 120. Charger, earthenware. Burmantofts Faience (J. Wilcock). Diameter 10½ins. Circa 1885.

Figure 121. Vase, earthenware.
Burmantofts Faience (J. Wilcock).
Height 8¾ins. Circa 1905.

Figure 122. Vase, earthenware. Burmantofts Faience (J. Wilcock).
Height 6¼ins. Circa 1905.

Figure 123. Vase, earthenware. Burmantofts Faience (J. Wilcock). Height 7ins. Circa 1905.

Figure 124. Vase, earthenware. Bretby Art Pottery (H. Tooth). Height 12½ins. Circa 1885.

Figure 125. Vase, earthenware. Bretby Art Pottery (H. Tooth). Height 22ins. Circa 1885.

Figure 126. Vase, earthenware. Bretby Art Pottery (H. Tooth). Height 13ins. Circa 1895.

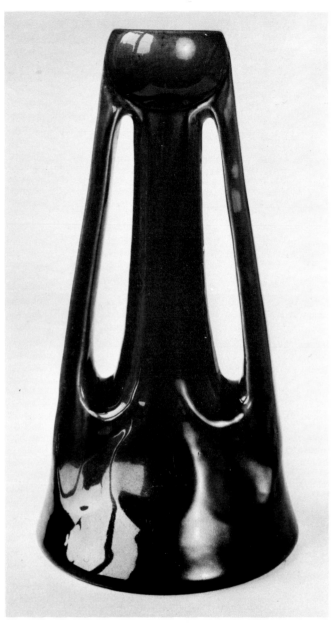

Figure 128. Vase, earthenware. Bretby Art Pottery (H. Tooth). Height 15½ins. Circa 1895.

Figure 127. Vase, earthenware. Bretby Art Pottery (H. Tooth). Height 12ins. Circa 1895.

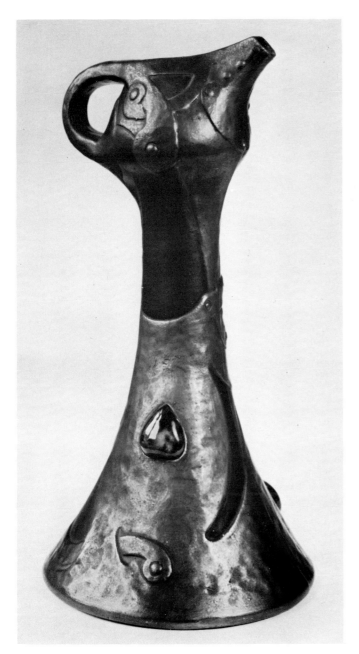

Figure 130. Vase, earthenware. Bretby Art Pottery (H. Tooth). Height 5¼ins. Circa 1900.

Figure 129. Ewer, earthenware. Bretby Art Pottery (H. Tooth). Height 12½ins. Circa 1900.

Figure 132. Vase, earthenware. William Ault, designed by Christopher Dresser. Height 6ins. Circa 1895.

Figure 131. Jug-vase, earthenware. Bretby Art Pottery (H. Tooth). Height 4ins. Circa 1885.

Figure 133. Vase, earthenware. William Ault, designed by Christopher Dresser. Height 8½ins. Circa 1895.

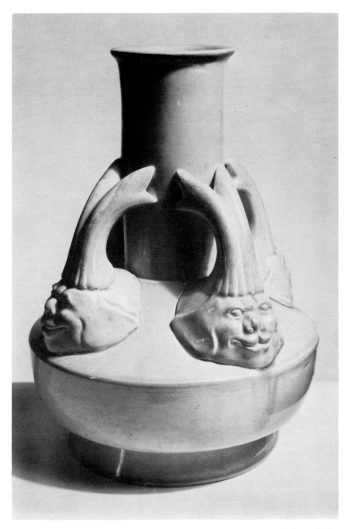

Figure 134. Vase, earthenware. William Ault, designed by Christopher Dresser. Height 9ins. Circa 1895.

Figure 135. Jug, earthenware. William Ault. Height 6¼ins. Circa 1890.

Figure 136. Vase, earthenware. William Ault, designed by Christopher Dresser (attributed), decorated by Clarissa J. Ault. Height 6¾ins. Circa 1900.

Figure 137. Vase, earthenware. Florian Ware (James Macintyre), designed by William Moorcroft. Height 10¾ins. Circa 1900.

Figure 138. Vase, earthenware. Florian Ware (James Macintyre), designed by William Moorcroft. Height 11½ins. Circa 1904.

Figure 139. Bonbonniere and cover, earthenware. James Macintyre, designed by William Moorcroft. Height 8¼ins. Circa 1905.

Figure 140. Tobacco-jar and cover, earthenware. James Macintyre, designed by William Moorcroft. Height 4ins. Circa 1905.

Figure 141. Vase, earthenware. Florian Ware (James Macintyre), designed by William Moorcroft. Height 10ins. Circa 1902.

Figure 142. Vase, earthenware. Flamminian Ware (James Macintyre), designed by William Moorcroft. Height 12½ins. Circa 1905.

Figure 143. Vase, earthenware. Pilkington's Tile and Pottery Co., designed by Walter Crane, decorated by Richard Joyce. Height 10¼ins. Dated 1907.

Figure 144. Vase, earthenware. Pilkington's Tile and Pottery Co., decorated by Richard Joyce. Height 8¼ins. Dated 1908.

Figure 145. Vase, earthenware. Pilkington's Tile and Pottery Co., decorated by Richard Joyce. Height 7¾ins. Dated 1911.

Figure 146. Vase, earthenware. Pilkington's Tile and Pottery Co., decorated by Richard Joyce. Height 8ins. Dated 1912.

Figure 147. Vase, earthenware. Pilkington's Tile and Pottery Co., decorated by W.S. Mycock. Height 8ins. Dated 1908.

Figure 148. Vase, earthenware. Pilkington's Tile and Pottery Co., decorated by W.S. Mycock. Height 9ins. Dated 1910.

Figure 149. Vase, earthenware. Pilkington's Tile and Pottery Co., decorated by W.S. Mycock. Height 9¼ins. Dated 1912.

Figure 150. Vase, earthenware. Pilkington's Tile and Pottery Co., decorated by W.S. Mycock. Height 7ins. Dated 1913.

Figure 151. Box and cover, earthenware. Pilkington's Tile and Pottery Co., decorated by G. Rodgers. Diameter 4ins. Dated 1908.

Figure 152. Jar and cover, earthenware. Pilkington's Tile and Pottery Co., decorated by G. Rodgers. Height 9¼ins. Circa 1920.

Figure 153. Vase, earthenware. Pilkington's Tile and Pottery Co., decorated by Gordon Forsyth. Height 17¼ins. Dated 1909.

Figure 154. Vase, earthenware. Pilkington's Tile and Pottery Co., decorated by Gordon Forsyth. Height 6¾ins. Dated 1912.

Figure 155. Bowl, earthenware. Alfred and Louise Powell, decorated by Louise Powell. Diameter 8ins. Circa 1910.

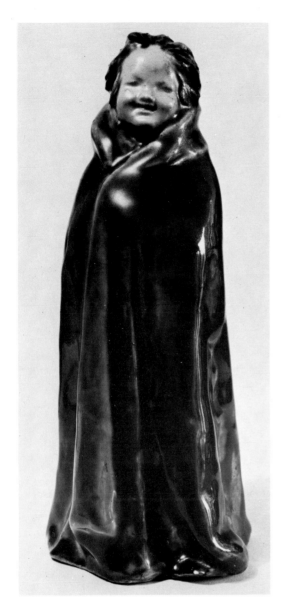

Figure 156. Figure, stoneware. Phoebe Stabler.
Height 7½ins. Dated 1915.

Figure 157. Vase, earthenware. Doulton Flambé (Doulton and
Co.). Height 6½ins. Circa 1910.

Figure 158. Vase, earthenware. Doulton Flambé (Doulton and Co.). Height 5¼ins. Circa 1910.

Figure 159. Vase, earthenware. Doulton Flambé (Doulton and Co.). Height 7¾ins. Circa 1910.

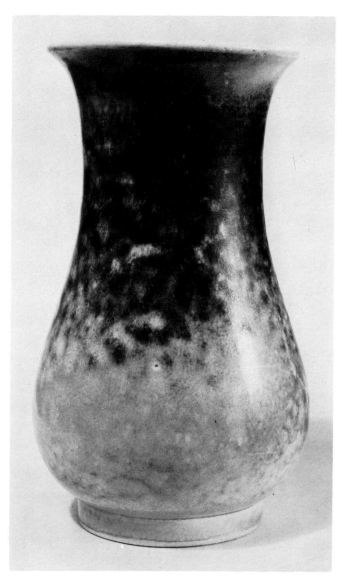

Figure 160. Vase, porcelain. Bernard Moore. Height 5½ins. Circa 1910.

Figure 161. Vase, porcelain. Bernard Moore. Height 5¾ins. Circa 1910.

Figure 162. Vase, porcelain. Bernard Moore. Height 6ins. Circa 1910.

Figure 163. Vase, porcelain. Bernard Moore. Height 5½ins. Circa 1910.

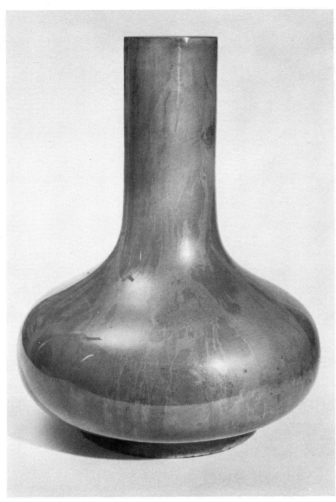

Figure 164. Vase, earthenware. Howson. Height 9¾ins. Dated 1912.

Figure 165. Vase, earthenware. G.L. Ashworth & Bros. Height 7¾ins. Circa 1910.

Figure 167. Vase, earthenware. Ruskin Pottery (W.H. Taylor). Height 9½ins. Dated 1905.

Figure 166. Vase, earthenware. Ruskin Pottery (W.H. Taylor). Height 7½ins. Dated 1905.

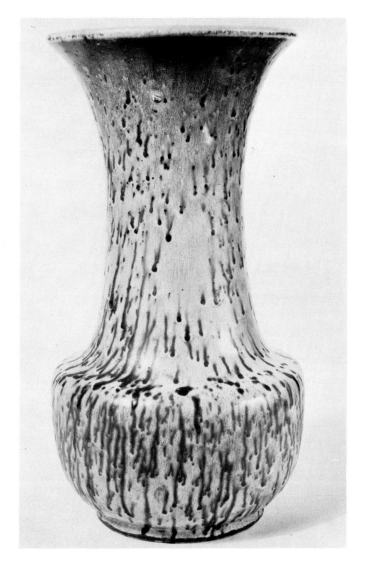

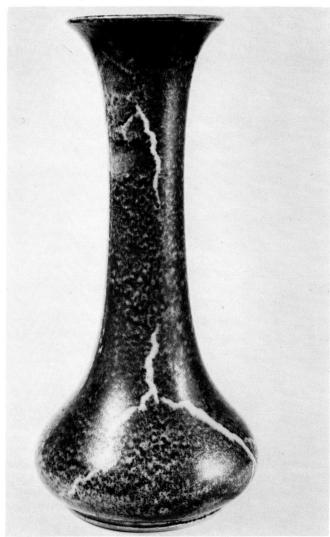

Figure 168. Vase, earthenware. Ruskin Pottery (W.H. Taylor).
Height 12¼ins. Dated 1908.

Figure 169. Vase, earthenware. Ruskin Pottery (W.H. Taylor).
Height 14¾ins. Dated 1909.

Figure 171. Vase, earthenware. Ruskin Pottery (W.H. Taylor). Height 4½ins. Dated 1910.

Figure 170. Vase, earthenware. Ruskin Pottery (W.H. Taylor). Height 8½ins. Dated 1922.

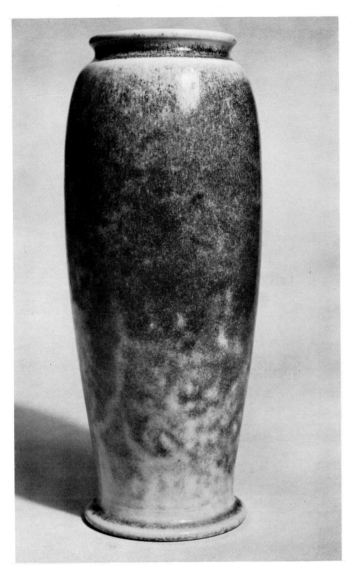

Figure 172. Vase, earthenware. Ruskin Pottery (W.H. Taylor). Height 9½ins. Dated 1912.

Figure 173. Vase, earthenware. Ruskin Pottery (W.H. Taylor). Height 6¼ins. Dated 1925.

Figure 175. Bowl and cover, earthenware. Ruskin Pottery (W.H. Taylor). Diameter 4½ins. Circa 1910.

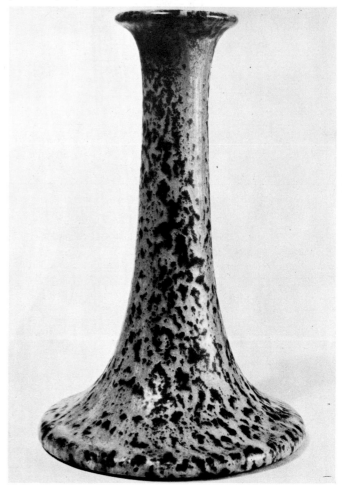

Figure 174. Vase, earthenware. Ruskin Pottery (W.H. Taylor). Height 9¼ins. Dated 1924.

Figure 176. Candlestick, earthenware. Ashby Potters' Guild. Height 6¼ins. 1909-22.

Figure 177. Bowl, earthenware. Carter & Co. Diameter 5½ins. Circa 1910.

Figure 178. Vase, earthenware. Carter & Co. Height 8½ins. Circa 1915.

Figure 179. Jar and cover, earthenware. Carter and Co. Height 5¾ins. Circa 1914.

Figure 180. Jar and cover, earthenware. Carter and Co. Height 8¼ins. Circa 1912.

Figure 181. Vase, earthenware. Pilkington's Tile and Pottery Co. Height 12¾ins. Circa 1900.

Figure 182. Vase, earthenware. Pilkington's Tile and Pottery Co. Height 7½ins. Circa 1905.

Figure 183. Vase, earthenware. Pilkington's Tile and Pottery Co. Height 6¼ins. Circa 1905.

Figure 184. Vase, earthenware. Pilkington's Tile and Pottery Co. Height 8ins. Circa 1905.

Figure 185. Vase, earthenware. Salopian Art Pottery Co. Height 9½ins. Circa 1905.

Figure 186. Vase, earthenware. Salopian Art Pottery Co. Height 8½ins. Circa 1905.

Figure 187. Vase, earthenware. Salopian Art Pottery Co. Height 5½ins. Circa 1905.

Figure 188. Vase, earthenware. Edmund Elton. Height 7¾ins.
Circa 1910.

Figure 189. Vase, earthenware. Edmund Elton. Height 7½ins.
Circa 1910.

Figure 191. Jug, earthenware. Edmund Elton. Height 3¼ins. Circa 1910.

Figure 190. Vase, earthenware. Edmund Elton. Height 5¼ins. Circa 1910.

Figure 192. Vase, earthenware. Edmund Elton. Height 4ins. Circa 1910.

*Figure 194. Jug, stoneware. Martin Brothers. Height 6ins.
Dated 1895.*

*Figure 193. Vase, earthenware. Edmund Elton. Height 7ins.
Circa 1910.*

Figure 195. Vase, Stoneware. Martin Brothers. Height 9½ins. Dated 1903.

Figure 196. Vase, stoneware. Martin Brothers. Height 5ins. Dated 1907

Figure 197. Vase, stoneware. Martin Brothers. Height 6¼ins. Dated 1907.

Figure 198. Vase, stoneware. Martin Brothers. Height 6ins. Dated 1911.

*Figure 199. Vase, stoneware. Martin Brothers. Height 11ins.
Dated 1911.*

*Figure 200. Vase, earthenware. Coldrum Pottery (Reginald F.
Wells). Height 7ins. Circa 1915.*

Figure 201. Vase, earthenware. Coldrum Pottery (Reginald F. Wells). Height 7¾ins. Dated 1910.

Figure 202. Vase, earthenware. Mortlake Pottery (George J. Cox). Height 10¾ins. Dated 1912.

Figure 203. Vase, earthenware. Mortlake Pottery (George J. Cox). Height 7¼ins. Dated 1912.

Figure 204. Vase, earthenware. Upchurch Pottery. Height 7½ins. Circa 1915.

Figure 205. Vase, earthenware. Upchurch Pottery. Height 12¾ins. Circa 1915.

1.   *ALLER VALE POTTERIES, Newton Abbott, Devon, 1887-1901. Impressed mark.*

2.   *C.J.C. BAILEY, Fulham Pottery, London, 1864-89. Impressed and incised marks.*

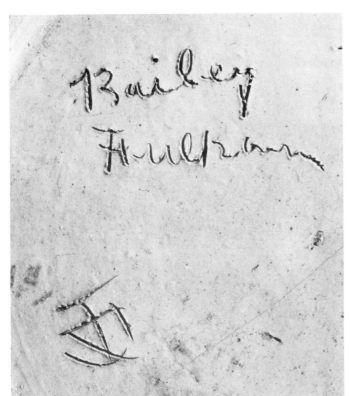

3,4.　*C.J.C. BAILEY, Fulham Pottery, London, 1864-89. Impressed and incised marks. (4) shows rebus and initials of Edgar Kettle.*

5.　*C.H. BRANNAM, Barnstaple, Devon, 1879- . Typical incised mark, including artist's monogram 'J.D.' for James Dewdney.*

6.   *BRETBY ART POTTERY (H. Tooth), Woodville, near Burton-on-Trent, 1887- .*
Impressed mark.

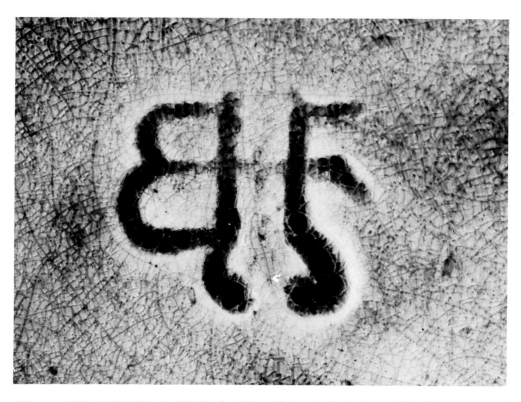

7-9.   *BURMANTOFTS FAIENCE (J. Wilcock), Leeds, Yorkshire, 1880-1904. Impressed*
marks and painted monogram of unidentified artist (9).

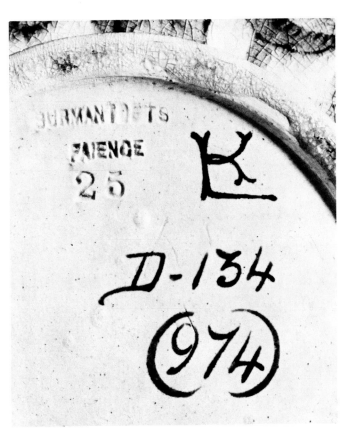

7-9.   *BURMANTOFTS FAIENCE (J. Wilcock), Leeds, Yorkshire, 1880-1904. Impressed marks and painted monogram of unidentified artist (9).*

10.   *COLDRUM POTTERY (Reginald F. Wells), West Malling, Kent, and Chelsea, London, circa 1908-1924. Impressed mark.*

11.   *CARTER & CO., Poole, Dorset, 1873-1921. Impressed mark*

12,13. *CRAVEN DUNNILL & CO., Jackfield, Shropshire, 1872-1951.*
Impressed marks.

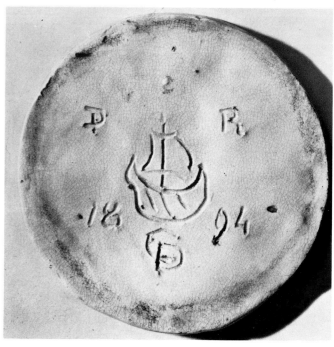

14. **WILLIAM DE MORGAN,** *Chelsea, Merton Abbey*
and Fulham, London, circa 1872-1907. One of
several impressed marks, and painted initials of the
artist Fred Passenger.

15. **DELLA ROBBIA POTTERY,** *Birkenhead, Cheshire,*
1894-1906. Incised mark, and monogram of Conrad
Dressler, designer and modeller.

16.   *Impressed mark on stoneware, circa 1880-1902.*   17.   *Impressed mark, circa 1902-22.*

18.   *Printed mark on Faience, from circa 1872.*   19.   *Impressed mark on Impasto, from circa 1879.*

16-20.   DOULTON   &   CO.,   Lambeth,   London,   circa   1858-1956.

20.   *DOULTON & CO., Lambeth, London, circa 1858-1956. Impressed mark on Silicon from circa 1880.*

21.   *DOULTON & CO., Burslem, Staffordshire, 1882- . Printed mark used from circa 1902, with FLAMBÉ added for* flambé *glazed wares from circa 1905.*

22.   *SIR EDMUND ELTON, Sunflower Pottery, Clevedon, Somerset. Painted mark (date rarely found).*

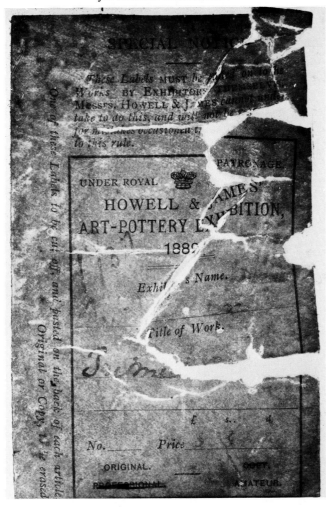

HOWELL & JAMES'
SPECIAL MAKE

23.   HOWELL & JAMES, Regent St., London, circa 1820-1922. Retailers. Printed mark on blank sold
for amateur decoration.

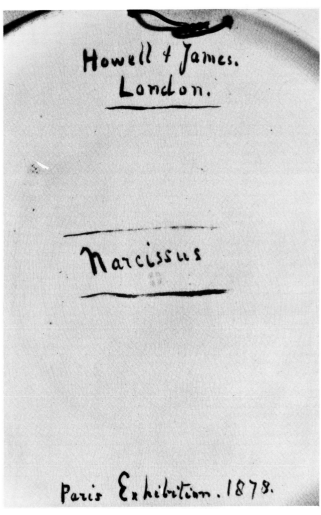

24.   HOWELL & JAMES, Regent St., London, circa
1820-1922. Retailers. Label on piece entered for
annual Art-Pottery Exhibition.

25.   HOWELL & JAMES, Regent St., London, circa
1820-1922. Retailers. Painted mark on piece shown
at the Paris Exhibition of 1878.

26. *ALEXANDER LAUDER, Barnstaple, Devon, 1876-1914. Typical incised mark.*

27. *LINTHORPE POTTERY, Middlesbrough, Yorkshire, 1879-89. Impressed marks, including facsimile signature of Christopher Dresser.*

28,29. *MARTIN BROTHERS, Fulham and Southall, London, 1873-1914. (28) Incised mark of Robert Wallace Martin from the period before the brothers established their pottery at Southall. (29) Typical incised mark 1877-1914.*

30.   MINTON'S ART-POTTERY STUDIO, Kensington
Gore, London, 1871-75. Printed mark.

31.   WILLIAM MOORCROFT, Burslem, Staffordshire,
1897-1945. Painted signature on piece of Florian
Ware. (Manufactured by J. Macintyre & Co. Ltd.).

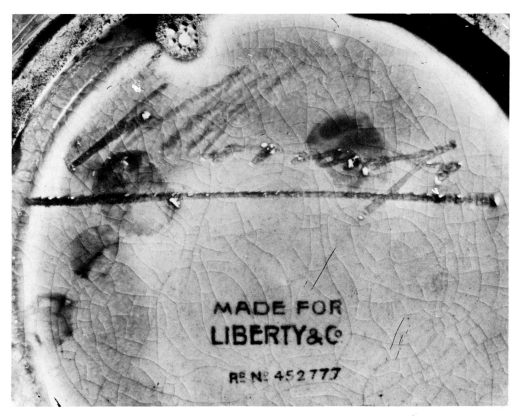

32.   WILLIAM MOORCROFT, Burslem, Staffordshire, 1897-1945. Painted signature on
piece of Flamminian Ware. (Manufactured by J. Macintyre & Co. Ltd.).

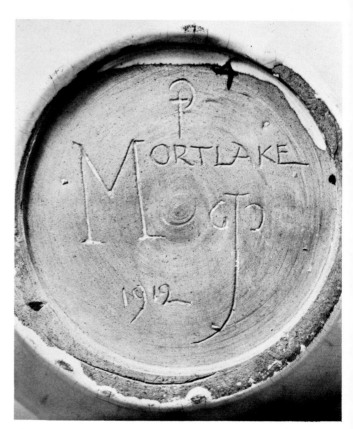

33.   *BERNARD MOORE, Stoke Staffordshire, 1905-15.*
Painted mark.

34.   *MORTLAKE POTTERY, Mortlake, London, circa*
1911-circa 1915. Incised mark, with incised mono-
gram of George J. Cox.

35.   *JOHN PEARSON, London, circa 1890-circa 1900. Painted monogram. The devices,*
on this piece a fish, varied.

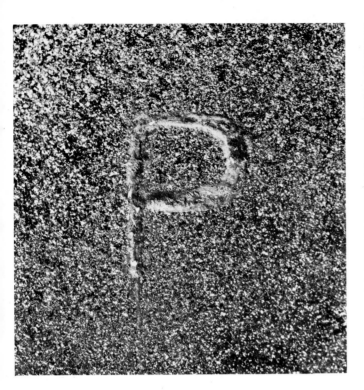

36,37. *PILKINGTON'S TILE AND POTTERY CO., Clifton Junction, near Manchester, Lancashire, 1893-1938 and 1948-57. (36) Impressed mark, circa 1900. (37) Impressed mark, circa 1905-14, with painted monogram of W.S. Mycock. Roman numeral VIII denotes 1908.*

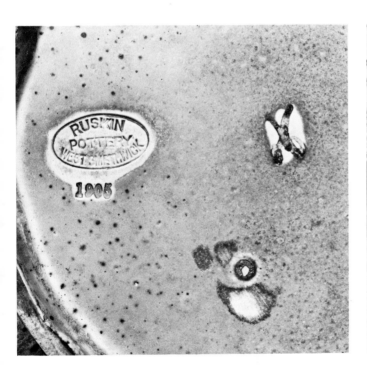

38,39. *RUSKIN POTTERY, West Smethwick, Birmingham, 1898-1933. Impressed marks. The painted scissors (38) are a rebus for W.H. Taylor.*

40. *SALOPIAN ART POTTERY CO., Benthall, near Broseley, Shropshire, 1882-circa 1912. Impressed mark.*

41. *UPCHURCH POTTERY, Rainham, Kent, 1913-61. Impressed mark.*

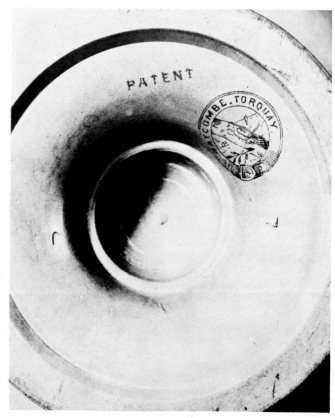

42. *WATCOMBE POTTERY CO., St. Mary Church, Devon, 1867-1901. Printed mark. On some pieces, only the impressed arrowhead mark appears.*